ENLIGHTENED

ENLIGHTENED

Seven Chakras to Self-Discovery

ANNEMARIE HECKERT

ST. MARTIN'S
ESSENTIALS
NEW YORK

First published in the United States by St. Martin's Essentials, an imprint of St. Martin's Publishing Group

ENLIGHTENED. Copyright © 2024 by Annemarie Heckert. All rights reserved. Printed in the United States of America. For information, address St. Martin's Publishing Group, 120 Broadway, New York, NY 10271.

www.stmartins.com

Designed by Steven Seighman

The Library of Congress Cataloging-in-Publication Data is available upon request.

ISBN 978-1-250-88680-4 (trade paperback)
ISBN 978-1-250-88681-1 (ebook)

Our books may be purchased in bulk for promotional, educational, or business use. Please contact your local bookseller or the Macmillan Corporate and Premium Sales Department at 1-800-221-7945, extension 5442, or by email at MacmillanSpecialMarkets@macmillan.com.

First Edition: 2024

10 9 8 7 6 5 4 3 2 1

This book is dedicated to my children.
You are my love, my light.

&

To my mother, Theresa, and my father, James, for planting
me firmly in the ground. To my sister, Jennifer, and my
brother, James, for growing with me. To Aunt Betty Lou
and Candy Danzis, who believed as I blossomed.

All my gratitude to the incredibly talented team and my
editor, Joel Fotinos, at Macmillan, St. Martin's Press, for
going out on a limb and over the rainbow. And to my
beloved clients for your unwavering patience as I move
between Heaven and Earth, *thank you.*

CONTENTS

FOREWORD

Author Annemarie Heckert experienced a mystical awakening, where an eternal switch into the Infinite was flipped. A vocation she never knew she wanted called her courageously forward into the unknown. Talk about a scary mission! It was goodbye to a conventional life and hello to a sacred, spiritual unfolding.

Her debut book, *Enlightened*, explores with tremendous vulnerability her personal journey of learning, healing, and letting go, along with all the magical blessings that arrived, right on time, as a result. Her courage, humility, and grace, and all the lessons she shares along the way, are guideposts for cutting the brush of a brand-new road—a fresh road that may be beckoning you forward right now.

The Chakras, locations of specific inner radiance, can often seem mysterious and confusing. I see them artistically rendered on everything from wall hangings to coffee mugs to T-shirts. Yet when I talk with others about them, there seems to be much bewilderment. Your Author to the rescue! How Annemarie explains the Chakras here dispels the confusion like the sun piercing through the clouds. I love this! She makes working with our own Chakras both easy and practical, providing grounding to the etheric. Annemarie bravely uses her own narrative, along with those of her clients, to weave a deeper understanding of Chakra wisdom and how it can benefit us all. The information shared here will be very valuable for both energy healing newbies and experienced practitioners alike.

I never wanted to be an Energy Healer. Or rather, I never even had the thought that I could be—and how can you desire something you don't even realize is possible? All I ever truly wanted was to be happy, so I followed the "still, small voice" within. This led me to books, spiritual teachers, and practices that turned everything I thought I knew inside out, while somehow revealing what I intuitively knew all along. What I learned and experienced joined forces with my natural empathetic sensitivity and the "divine downloads" I'd experienced since I was a child. Dormant talents and abilities were awakened within me, rising to be seen and used. This both shocked and delighted me.

Now, as an international energy healer and author of three books, my happiness and bliss are as much my guides as my angels and ancestors. No conventional journey could have ever provided this much fulfillment. Not for me. Not for most of us.

You may have heard the often-used expression, "the road less traveled," born from the title of that famous book by M. Scott Peck, which in turn had been inspired by the beautiful poem by Robert Frost. This statement encourages us to forgo checking the boxes of the well-worn path for a "regular life" like following a recipe. Instead, it encourages us to choose direction from our inner callings, beckoning us forward. Life itself is whispering the directions for our own personal joy. If *Enlightened* could have a second subtitle, *The Road Never Traveled Before* would be most fitting.

Enlightened will be a wonderful guide to connect you to your own inherent spiritual nature. I fully believe the challenges of modern life are offering us opportunities to remember who we truly are—not just bodies that will fade and transition, but infinite souls that are eternal. We have so much more power within us! *Enlightened* will be a wonderful guide for us to grow, serve, create, and remember. After all, as a meme I once saw said, "Not all questions can be answered by Google."

Wishing you many blessings on your journey!

—Kris Ferraro

International Energy Healer and bestselling author of *Manifesting, Your Difference Is Your Strength,* and *Energy Healing*

Dear Reader,

Thank you for choosing to read this book. My intention is that you will see a glimpse into the role of a Medium, the myriad of complex relationships we have on this Earth and in Heaven, and how our experiences and relationships shape our own enlightenment through the chakras. While I may be a gifted clairvoyant, the stories in this book are compressed into generalized adaptations and not intended for specific determinations or diagnoses. I am not formally medically trained and encourage you to seek professional medical care should you feel called to do so. I have learned that spirituality is expressed in many forms, that healers and teachers come in many shapes, and that miracles come in all sizes.

Some names, identifying details, characters, businesses or places, events or incidents have been changed, and in some instances compounded, to protect the privacy of those who have inspired this book.

I invite you to share in an opening prayer with me, as I do with every reading. In this prayer, I call upon the archangels to uplift and support us as we dedicate this book, now a sacred space, to witness the many lessons through the chakras toward enlightenment and eternal life.

Love,
Annemarie

For God so loved the world that he gave his one and only Son, that whoever believes in him shall not perish but have eternal life.

—JOHN 3:16

INVOCATION

Beloved Mother, Father God,

Thank you for allowing this alignment today.

Thank you to Archangel Michael, for clearing all energy that no longer serves us.

Thank you to Archangel Muriel, for your balanced emotions.

Thank you to Archangel Jophiel, for your joy, your laughter.

Thank you to Archangel Raphael, for your healing light.

Thank you to Archangel Gabrielle, for your clear communication.

Thank you to Archangel Uriel, for your wisdom and clarity.

Thank you to Archangel Zadkiel, for your grace and your ease through all transitions.

This is now a sacred space for all who enter.

Amen.

MY ROOTS

I believe that a history of the human experience is best expressed not through edict but through story. Through careful consideration and with the utmost respect, I have painstakingly selected the following stories to share with you from the collection of thousands I have witnessed, firsthand, as a messenger between Heaven and Earth: a clairvoyant Medium.

As I approached my work, I was downright resistant at first. I discovered that while I was sharing messages from Heaven with my clients, the messages were necessary and relevant to my own healing, as well. Now, as I offer them to you, it is my greatest hope that you, too, will align with these incredible stories as told through the winding pathways of the chakras.

The pathways of the chakras remind me of the roots of trees. My roots, my family, have been deeply influential with how I was led, or called, to become a Medium. With this book, you will see how the mature tree, now strengthened by expansive roots, was once a sapling susceptible to storms, and a sapling was once a seed, resting dormant in the dark.

My family tree—my mother, Theresa, and my father, James—had both been born with a resiliency and tenacity inherited by them through generations of fighters. And with those qualities, so too did they receive their own sixth senses: my mother a deeply empathic healer and clairsentient and my father, a warrior and clairaudient—who while in combat as a United States Marine listened to the guidance of his guardian angels to save his life. My grandmothers, Rita and Kate, were both blessed with claircognizance, or, as Kate would say, "I just *know* things." I grew up hearing stories of my great-grandmother and my namesake, Anna, for her clairvoyance. As Mommom Rita would say about her mother, "She had *the gifts*." By the time I was born, I suppose I was the next in line to receive the gifts. But, I did not receive just one. I received them all.

I was told the story of my birth by my grandmother Kate, who narrated with her smoker-stained gravelly voice, gliding back and forth in her old brown rocking chair by her kitchen windows. She kept a notepad and pencil on a pedestal table that doubled as a floor lamp with *National Enquirer* magazines strewn into a basket on the floor. An antique, heavy dry sink sat behind her where Mr. Coffee percolated pot after pot of dark black coffee every morning and afternoon.

"Your sister . . . Your sister stood right there at that door for three days, cryin', until you got here," she said, pointing to the back door.

"Why was she cryin'?" I asked, seated at her kitchen table eating a Lebanon bologna sandwich after school. I had stopped by Grandma Kate's house to bring up the mail, take down the trash, and sweep the back porch—common chores for me since my older sister, Jenny, had left for college.

"Because she wanted your mother, and your father was

away working!" she said impatiently, as though I should have known.

One might expect that the way in which a baby is born unto the Earth does not matter entirely or presuppose the true nature of the child's value or worthiness of love, but from the time I arrived, it seemed as though I had been intruding upon a way of living that, for generations, had remained undisturbed.

Despite my sister, Jenny, being just seventeen months older than me, I often felt like an outsider. At the time of my birth, she was a beautiful little girl with fawn-shaped blue eyes and long, angelic curly hair that bounced and covered her eyes when she played. And apparently, from what Grandma Kate recalled, she had rarely left Mom's side.

When I was born, on a cold, gray November afternoon in 1976, Mom and Dad had recently bought their first home: the Blue Hill School House, about twenty minutes away from Grandma Kate's house, in Dover, Pennsylvania. The small town of Dover is about two hours west of Philadelphia and thirty minutes south of Harrisburg down the river. The Susquehanna River Valley has large, multigenerational family farms that sweep over the gently rolling hills and deeply wooded forests. The Blue Hill School House was originally a one-room schoolhouse but had recently been converted into a home with a loft and one small bedroom. There was a square porch out front that overlooked a dirt road lined with tall spruce, hemlock, and maple trees. Inside, without household furniture, one might mistake the house for a church, with its long, wide-plank hardwood floors that echoed footsteps across the sparsely furnished home.

There was a massive stone fireplace that was our sole source of heat and a deep white kitchen sink where stacked dishes would rest until Mom could get to them. She worked as a secretary for Appleton Papers and Dad had recently gotten out of the Marine Corps, Vietnam, and the Harrisburg, Pennsylvania, Fire Department as a fireman when we lived at the schoolhouse.

It was at this home that I call to mind one of my first interactions with my guardian angels. I have always had an excellent memory, for which I am grateful, because aside from it, I have struggled with almost everything else. One cold spring evening when I was about five months old, as Mom busied herself with my sister and cooking dinner, she had placed me in my high chair not too far from the fireplace. As I sat there, Mom's return had taken a bit longer than usual, and the fire had become hotter and hotter. I could feel my cheeks turn rosy and sweat started to bead at my brow. Although I was safe, my guardian angel drifted closer to me and quietly waited for Mom to return. I was peaceful, although a bit frustrated that I had been left unattended by the fire.

As I grew to be a toddler, the angels never left my side. In fact, I remember swinging from my baby swing while Mom pulled weeds around the square front porch and seeing my angels huddled around the schoolhouse's front door and me. I saw them as plainly as I saw my mother. My angels were harmoniously ever-present.

My parents, sister, and I didn't stay at the Blue Hill School House long. By the time I was two, we had made our first of nine moves. First, to Nashville, Georgia, where Dad was hired as a hunting dog trainer at a local plantation—a passion of his since childhood. Mom and Dad bought a beautiful A-frame house that sat down a red-clay road lined with pine trees and azaleas. I had a best friend, Lily, across the street and a sandbox out back. Mom had decorated the bedroom Jenny and I shared in pink-and-white buffalo-check linens and curtains. Teddy bears and dolls lined our bed and sunshine poured in through the windows that were protected by the tall pines out front.

It was at our home in Nashville that I was first introduced to fear. Mom had started a fire in the family room fireplace with fresh green pine needles and a chimney fire broke out. Our family room quickly filled with smoke, and plumes of hot, gray ash swelled into the carpet, the sofa, the air, and my eyes.

Jenny and I were charged with racing to and from the kitchen sink to fill mixing bowls with water. When the fire became too hot to tolerate, Mom called for Dad, who brought the garden hose in from outside and put out the flames. My guardian angel kept Jenny and me aside and spoke to me calmly over my father's loud directions. It was a difficult and confusing moment to watch. Was it the fire or Dad's volume that rattled my peace and our home? Until that point, I had not seen or heard anyone yell quite like my father did that evening, but the fire got extinguished, and we were all safe again.

In our next home, in Monticello, Florida, there was no fireplace. Next, we had a ranch-style house with a cement driveway and a garage where I stored my first bicycle with training wheels. Dogwood trees bloomed pink and white as far into the back woods as I could see. Mom warned me not to play too close to the red-ant mounds out front that, to a four-year-old, were as threatening as a minefield. Instead, Mom and I sat on the blue carpet indoors in front of our oversized TV to play with Legos and watch *Sesame Street* while Jenny was at school. Although I was four, our rural community did not have a preschool, and between the woods and the ants outside, I was often on my own indoors.

We had a small free-standing keyboard tucked into the corner of the guest bedroom in Monticello. I was standing to read the notes while matching them to the keys, when the temperature dropped in the bedroom. I felt a coolness in the room and looked over my shoulder to see that a man had entered the bedroom and sat down, quietly, on the spare bed. I had not heard a knock on the front door or Mom welcoming a guest. But I stood there politely, wondering who he was. He was dressed in dirty clothes with soot on his face and shoulders and what looked like a cowboy-style hat in his hands. He was not a big man, although his posture was hunched over, and I could feel an overwhelming sadness. Nervously, I nodded at him, but he did not respond. So, I played my favorite song, "Twinkle, Twinkle, Little Star," on the keyboard for him. Again, he sat without acknowledging me, so I mustered up my voice, put my hand on my hip, and said, "I played you a song. Aren't you gonna clap?"

He turned his head to face me and said, "I can't."

"And why not?" I prodded.

"Because I'm stuck," he replied.

At that moment, the temperature seemed to dip even cooler, and the weight of his sadness overwhelmed the back bedroom beyond what I could handle. Although he sat between me and the door, I darted past him out to the kitchen and alerted Mom that there was a stranger in the spare bedroom.

Alarmed, Mom confidently walked down the hall to see for herself, but no one was there.

"No one is there, Annie," she said. "It's just the bed and keyboard."

It wasn't until many years later that I pieced together my first experience seeing and speaking with a spirit. From that day on at the ranch house in Monticello, occurrences like this happened regularly. So much so that I began having trouble being by myself or falling asleep.

Mom voiced her concerns to Dad one day that bedtime had become increasingly difficult for me, so they moved their record player into my bedroom, hoping that the songs would lull me to sleep. I quickly learned that by listening to music to fall asleep, I could buffer out the interruptions from spirits or angels bustling through my bedroom—or worse, under my bed. This strategy of using music to temper spirits and angels helped me immensely to feel safe and not become overwhelmed by the constant activity.

Dad was often away working, and without prior knowing, I would frequently see glimpses of him in my mind's eye. He was tall and athletic, with coal-black hair and steely gray-blue eyes, and I was always delighted to see him in my mind. In person, he was so removed from our day-to-day routine that Mom had to tell him where my kindergarten was on more than one occasion! I thought at the time that my visions of Dad were by my own doing. Perhaps my own imagination. I could not have known that it was the very first psychic and remote viewing I would ever experience.

Mom was an exceptionally beautiful woman as a young mother—and still is. With blonde hair and blue eyes, a petite frame, and gentle demeanor, Mom always spoke softly and kindly to Jenny and me. Oftentimes, at grocery stores or while shopping, complete strangers would stop us and ask if she was on TV or had been in the movies. She had an innocent heart and a glow about her, for sure.

In the summer before my second-grade year, Dad, Mom, Jenny, and I moved again: this time to a plantation with thousands of acres of red-dirt roads, more pine trees than stars in the sky, and plenty of ponds for fishing on the outskirts of Albany, Georgia. Dad worked as the general manager of a plantation as well as the host of routine upland game bird hunts. Before he had volunteered for the Marine Corps, the outdoors, bird dogs, and horses had provided a welcome refuge to him, as he struggled with dyslexia in school. By the time Dad was in his early thirties, he returned to train bird dogs professionally and had proven himself to be quite a competitor. In this time-old tradition, Dad became an expert in his field and well respected in the hunting and bird dog community in the South and all over the country. We lived in Albany for just four years, but it was there that I went to St. Teresa's Catholic School and had my first formal introduction to religion, spirituality, and angels.

I loved everything about St. Teresa's School. I felt right at home with the morning prayers led by Sister Pauline, holy day masses, and statues and paintings of saints and angels interspersed throughout the corridors and courtyards. By my fifth-grade year, Dad and Mom had welcomed my baby brother, Jimmy, into the world and for a while, we were a peaceful family with evening supper around the kitchen table, a happy yellow Labrador named Shadow at our feet, and best friends and birthday parties. These happy years, although short, would be the foundation we would lean back on in the challenging years to come.

As I continued to grow, we moved several more times before returning to Dad's hometown back in central Pennsylvania. Of course, I did not know it then, but my experiences with angels pressed on to include more and more "downloads" of information about the people around me, physical sensations about their health or illnesses, and predictive dreams and images.

It was a lot of information, *all* the time, and I found a typical day at school to be exhausting. I began to struggle with self-confidence as I saw my peers excelling in their academics while I just barely got by—especially in mathematics. I did everything I knew in order to succeed until about my senior year of high school, when I became so saddened to accept that even my best efforts at good grades were simply not enough.

Dad and Mom had drifted into a season of shifts as well, and arguments erupted at home. With Jimmy in elementary school and Jenny off to college, I took solace in art, music, and athletics, which, unbeknownst to me at the time, were the perfect remedy for balance and grounding—strategies that would show up for me again and again as invitations to keep exploring. What I did not realize then was that my angels, without any earthly instructors or coursework, were already giving me the foundation necessary for me to successfully receive and maintain their guidance—for myself and others.

Without ever knowing it, Dad and Mom were the perfect parents for me. At home, Dad disciplined with thunder and lightning and insisted on maintaining attention to detail, a constant alertness and situational awareness. To this day, I have yet to meet another person with such incredibly keen awareness. Mom, with her doe-like grace, offered absolute and unwavering forgiveness, compassion, and self-sacrifice to our family that has been unmatched by any other woman I have ever known. Now, as an adult, I have come to understand my parents as unique individuals moving through their own lessons, healing, and paths. What a sacred gift it has been for me to stand witness to their tribulations and triumphs. They have been, and continue to be, my greatest teachers. I see now how the seeds of their struggles were the taproot of my story as they sought security in a rupture-and-repair, nonlinear drive toward light both as individuals and as a couple.

As I began my path toward healing, it was as much an un-doing as it was a be-coming as I unpacked the narrative of my childhood and forged forward with a unique and autonomous rendering of what a grounded, healthy family felt like and looked like. The very definition by which my calling as a Medium challenged me, requiring that I leave it all behind—and rely entirely on my guidance from God and His angels.

ALLOW

Anna, my third and final baby, had just been born in the winter of 2011, when the rumblings of a distant storm began to reawaken my long-dormant gifts. A productive eighteen-year sabbatical of sorts away from the angels and spirit marched me through a four-year enlistment in the United States Navy, followed by four years of college where I earned a degree in English literature, marriage, moves, and three beautiful children of my own. By the summer after Anna arrived, I felt the winds of urgency pick up as I watched the poplar tree leaves turn upside down and storm clouds billow toward my home. It was as though God, the Universe, and all the angels had had just about enough of my avoidance. By the fall of that year, there was no turning back. Any semblance of a "normal" life slipped through my failed attempts like trying to open a faulty umbrella in a hurricane. It would be the beginning of my first surrender. Major turning points arise for me at, or around, my birth month of November as sure as the sun rises. The November of 2011 catapulted me into a series of shifts that would awaken me again and again, until I was brought to my knees.

My greatest dream was to have a big family, and as busy as I was with my son, Christopher, aged six, my daughter, Maria, aged two, and baby Anna, just six months old, I needed some time to myself. After months of breastfeeding baby Anna that was immediately preceded by breastfeeding and a pregnancy with Maria, I had not had any time to even take a deep breath, much less visit old friends. I planned a much-needed night on the town in Philadelphia for my thirty-fifth birthday, and my husband, Doyle, agreed to stay home with the children for the night.

I remember not knowing how to dress for the occasion—having stowed away the last of my maternity clothes and not fitting back into my pre-pregnancy clothes, I put on outdated blue jeans, a white T-shirt, and awkwardly draped a turquoise scarf around my shoulders, then cried as I kissed my babies goodbye for the evening. I looked forward to the two-hour drive to Center City to my friend Liz's apartment, where several friends who were coming in from New York and I had agreed to meet.

It was my first night out in almost three years and we carefully planned dinner, drinks, and pubs full of music. My thirty-fifth birthday in Philly was turning out to be everything I had hoped for. It was like a montage of snapshots from my sabbatical years. Friends from the Navy that felt more like family. Friends from my college years that love art, music, and wordsmithing. My past was right in front of me like a grand review of the joyful, adventurous, independent years I had before becoming a mother. We all met each other with hugs and kisses as though time had stood still. Our friendships and I had not skipped a beat—even though life had opened and expanded exponentially for me as a mother of three. I was the first of my friends to start a family and I had become a bit used to compartmentalizing my personal life from my social life, so I made sure to stay as present as possible that night, feeling all too well how infrequent these occasions were.

As we walked to our dinner reservations, we took a shortcut down Spruce Street and happened upon a psychic palm reader's small studio.

"I never knew this was here," my friend Liz said curiously, squinting inside.

"Let's go in!" said my friend Aaron from New York.

And just like that, Liz, Aaron, myself, and the rest of the crew all filed into the mystic's studio and our upbeat excitement was suppressed to a hush.

The studio was everything you would expect it to be. Incense sticks burning beyond the wooden holder, cheap tapestries hanging from the walls, stars and moons dangling from the ceiling like my daughter's crib mobile, crystal balls and tarot cards stacked up in the center of a small, circular table, draped in a fraying fabric. The mystic had kind eyes and spoke with an Eastern European accent. She gravitated right toward me and requested that everyone else wait outside.

"Fifteen minutes!" she said, waving her hands in the air. "Give me fifteen minutes!"

With that, she shooed my friends back outside and they giggled, while waiting patiently for me.

Up until this point in time, I had never had any kind of psychic reading. My only reference for a psychic was the character Oda Mae Brown played by Whoopi Goldberg in the movie *Ghost*. I had no idea what to expect and I was grateful I could still see my friends peering in the window from the sidewalk. She took a deep breath, prayed in her mother language, took my hands in hers, opened her eyes widely, and stared at my palms.

"Tell me your name three times," she said. As I began to speak, her eyes widened and with a sense of reverence, she shifted her posture and her tone of voice softened.

"Annemarie," she said. "Oh, Annemarie. This encounter today is no mistake. You have a very important message, and I am humbled to offer it to you on behalf of God and His angels. You are about to embark on a new life . . . and you will not be able to take anything you have known with you. It will be very difficult, but you will succeed. You and your children . . . you have three children . . . You and your children will always be together and safe. Always. But, you must go now and be brave. Be very brave, Annemarie. Your life was not meant to be a regular life. But first . . . you must heal yourself. You are here on this Earth to heal and to teach. You are enlightened. This is written."

As she spoke, I felt the walls of the small studio narrow, and although my friends were just outside, I could no longer see them. The smell of the incense was consuming, and I began to feel nauseous. She asked if I could stay longer, for more in-depth information, but I had received the message clearly, and took my hands out of hers and thanked her politely for her time. There was an unspoken knowing now, and I excused myself back outside where the cold November air hit my face with a shock.

"What'd she say, Annie?!" my friends asked, huddling around me, still carousing, as we began to walk again.

"What'd she say?!"

There were murmurings of, "You don't *really* believe in any of that stuff, do you?" and "Ahh, THAT was a waste of money!"

"Hey, Annie, gimme twenty bucks! I'LL TELL YOU YOUR FUTURE!" shouted my friend Joe, motioning to his crotch.

Shaking my head and rolling my eyes, I replied, "It was no big deal, guys. C'mon, let's get going."

My friends' shenanigans tempered my nerves some, but I couldn't help being somewhat intrigued by the mystic's message. Later that evening as I listened to the music, and watched as my fun-loving, loyal, and protective friends came together, I again tried to set aside the mystic's message and my years of avoidance. The pints of beer flowed and our late-night laughter echoed across Rittenhouse Square as we all walked together, arm in arm. A beautiful birthday . . . and, unbeknownst to me at the time, a farewell celebration to my life before.

I was fully prepared for a proper hangover the following morning as Liz made coffee and tidied up the remains of our night out. Friends were sprawled across her sofa, an air mattress, and the bedroom floor. I telephoned my children back home, then, equipped with sunglasses and extra-strength Tylenol, my friends and I headed out for a late breakfast before my two-hour return drive home. No one mentioned the stop at the mystic's again and I was content to fall back into the flow of babies, diapers, dishes, cooking, and cleaning surely awaiting my return home.

What I did not expect, however, was to experience the greatest spiritual experience of my life that day on my drive home: a Kundalini Awakening.

My route home on the Pennsylvania Turnpike was just 106 miles, from Philadelphia to Harrisburg. It is an easy drive and one that I had grown accustomed to over the years. The turnpike has small plazas interspersed for gas and pit stops, and about halfway home when I began to feel ill, I pulled my blue Saab 9–3 into a plaza and turned off the engine. As I sat, I waited for waves of nausea to subside. The nausea was like a warning signal for what was to come.

Internally, I felt as though I was vibrating, and as I sat still, the vibrations rose in intensity and frequency. I ran through a list of medical emergency symptoms. *Hangover? Food poisoning? Anxiety attack? Heart attack?* This was unlike anything I had ever known. *Is this a psychotic break?* I worried. For over two hours, I sat in complete silence and felt compelled to place my hands, facing with my palms open and upright, on each knee. I kept hearing, "Allow . . . allow . . . allow" over and over again in a deeply calm, peaceful voice. I felt like weeping, and jumbles of tangled emotions welled at the base of my throat. My breath slowed. I felt as though I was leaving my body and crystalline radiant light, anchored at my bottom, began to swirl and encircle within me and around me. It was of me, but not me. I was scared, but at peace. And I did my best to "allow." Never at any time did I feel as though I needed to ask for help or call an ambulance. I kept my eyes closed, but observed as the white light wrapped around my body and internal organs, gradually and gracefully spreading to my hips, my stomach, my heart, my throat, my hands and head. I felt for some time as though I had been given a crown and even raised my hand to ensure there was nothing physical resting on my head. I began hearing, "There are angels all around . . . There are angels all around . . . There are angels all around. Allow."

Of all the things that day, the presence of the angels did not surprise me, and I was grateful for their reassurance. As the sun set, I began to feel the heaviness of my body again. My feet. My core, softened by pregnancies. I took deep breaths and felt both energized and exhausted. I went into the restroom, finally, and washed my hands and splashed cold water on my face. I felt a deep sense of appreciation for my body and a need to forgive myself for ever having been critical or harsh to it. Even now, as I write this, I do not recall placing my feet on the ground, but kind of floating into the rest stop and the remainder of the drive home.

Turns out, the Spruce Street mystic was right. Nothing was ever the same.

THERE'S THAT WORD AGAIN

My first instinct was to schedule an appointment with my long-standing therapist. Since I was seventeen, I had routinely worked with a therapist—initially for support for my self-confidence around academics, but eventually for support for my marriage. I was so thankful for the counselors and psychologists that I'd worked with over the years, and kept them close as a network of confidantes and guides. But before I could get in with my therapist, a friend referred me to a Medium from Harrisburg, Pennsylvania: Maryanne Wellington. Maryanne had been a successful practicing Medium for twenty-five years and came highly recommended. Despite a typical waitlist of several months, I was scheduled for an appointment with her almost immediately.

Maryanne is a lovely woman, with a big smile and a warm, welcoming personality. Right away, I felt comfortable with her—partly because she was just not as "woo-woo" as the Spruce Street mystic. We met at an unmarked attorney's office where she subleased an office space, and we spent almost an hour in session together.

My first, burning question was, "What in the hell just happened to me, Maryanne?!" She smiled knowingly, like an experienced and wise professor from the Hogwarts School of Witchcraft and Wizardry in J. K. Rowling's Harry Potter series.

"Annemarie! Anne-mar-ie!" she said as she raised her pen in the air like a magic wand. "YOU are enlightened, my dear. You are a Medium and what you just experienced was a Kundalini Awakening!"

The word "enlightened" baffled me. "But Maryanne, in order to be enlightened . . . Don't you have to be a saint or something? I mean, I'm no Buddha. I'm just a regular person."

As Maryanne went on to share her own experiences with spirits and angels, I drifted off into thought, feeling grateful I finally had the validation and the key to unlock my lifetime of experiences—if even a bit tearful and relieved to know that I had not just experienced a psychotic episode. She immediately sent me on to two more teachers, and the path toward my work as a Medium began to unfold.

"You'll see, Annemarie. Everything will be all right, but I can tell you . . . You will never work a regular job again. Go now and learn everything you can about energy and the angels. You will be working with the angels!"

I began seeking a definition of enlightenment, of angels, and of a Kundalini Awakening. Although I had experienced an "awakening" myself, I was still hoping to find a frame of reference. Up until this point in my life, I had no training with energy-healing modalities, yoga practices, meditation, or ancient and Eastern philosophies. I had been raised a Catholic, and my knowledge beyond that was limited to a few comparative religion classes in college.

I learned that a Kundalini Awakening is likened to a powerful "coiled snake" of divine feminine energy or "Goddess" energy that rests at the base of the spine. When awakened, the energy winds up, within and around the root, sacral, solar plexus, heart, throat, third eye, and crown chakras, awakening and aligning the chakras toward enlightenment—which is precisely what I experienced.

I went on to learn that the Kundalini is associated with Hinduism and has been recognized in sacred texts for *thousands* of years. It is also associated with the goddesses of Bhairavi and Kubjika, and Parvati and Adi Parashakti, the supreme being in Shaktism.

Shaktism is believed to have existed before the onset of Buddhism, as far back as 9000 BC. The story says that the goddess

Shakti begins to rise, overcoming oppressed power and sexuality, and meets her divine masculine counterpart, Shiva, who represents consciousness. The activation that Shakti brings is intense, and is best when Shiva accompanies Shakti as a grounding force—discovering this made sense to me and I was able to tell a story of my experience to a few friends and family.

Shakti includes many goddesses within one, which I paralleled to be similar to Mother Mary and the saints. My introduction to Shakti and Shaktism was one of curiosity and excitement. If maybe a bit clumsy and certainly not academic, at first.

I felt like Spider-Man after he had gotten his new Spidey senses. If I had been "awakened" by "Goddess" energy, then why? And did it have to be along the Pennsylvania Turnpike!? How was I supposed to use this enlightened-ness? I needed to know more. After my reading with Maryanne Wellington, I took a few days to process all that had transpired. Maryanne gave me a definition and some direction, but I was still quite nervous, so I turned to my most trusted confidante. If Spider-Man had Aunt May, then I had Aunt Betty Lou.

It was a sunny morning in central Florida and Aunt Betty Lou was on her way to work in her silver BMW convertible roadster when I called her the following Monday. If the actress Goldie Hawn had a twin sister, it would be Aunt Betty Lou: a Fourth-of-July firework in a petite, blonde-haired, blue-eyed frame. Her can-do personality and our joy-filled conversations always uplifted me.

"Aunt Betty Lou? Do you have a minute?" I asked.

"Well, hello, sunshine! Hi, Annemarie, I sure do! What's happening?"

I began introducing the entire experience by asking her if she remembered stories of my great-grandmother, Anna, having *the gifts*.

"Oh, of course. My mom used to tell us about them all the time. Remember the story of the little bunny rabbit? Ha . . . I loved that story."

"Tell me that one. What happened?"

"Well, when your grandmother was a little girl, she and her seven siblings all lived on the farm in Pennsylvania down where St. Anthony of the Hills church is now. It was a beautiful farm and there were always ducks by the creek, horses and dogs. The farmhouse had a big front porch and several steps that led to the front door. Well, anyway, one day, Anna was on her way into the house after collecting the laundry on the line and paused to wait for a little bunny rabbit to scamper from the first step. She said, 'Now wait for the bunny to scoot,' but there was no bunny on the step. Oh, there were all kinds of stories just like that. Anna could see angels, too, just like she could see the spirits of the animals on the farm."

"Yep. I remember the stories that Mommom would share. Well, Aunt Betty Lou, I have to tell you that I have been seeing spirits and angels for a really long time, too. As long as I can remember. I just never had a reason to talk about it—until now."

And with that, I could feel her attention move from a wonderful memory to open-hearted compassion for my most recent experience as I shared with her the news. I had been fearful that no one aside from Maryanne would understand. I am sure my guardian angels prompted me to contact Aunt Betty Lou that morning, and she has been by my side ever since—as I began to discover, for myself, how to define and use this newly awakened enlightenment.

GOOD VIBRATIONS

For anyone that knows anything about spirituality, angels, spirits, and the like, the use of the term "life force energy" is as simple and as common as "bread, milk, and juice." It is so nonchalant that any educated person would say such a thing with effortlessness and ease. No big deal. But for me, my introduction to the vast vocabulary that had long escaped my awareness was another discovery that gave name to my newly claimed experiences. *Did the seven shepherds that discovered the Dead Sea Scrolls feel the same?* I wondered. Maryanne suggested that I meet with two teachers; first a Reiki Master Teacher and then a local Medium of angels named Candy Danzis.

By January of 2012, still a bit leery about what, exactly, I was to go learn and do, I registered for a Reiki One class. There, I was introduced to a more comprehensive vocabulary. New words like life force energy, prana, qi, and the chakras started coming into my awareness and I studied them carefully.

Life Force Energy is said to be a "vital force within all living things."

Prana goes back to some of the earliest texts, called the Upanishads. It is believed to be "the breath of life."

Qi (or chi) is rooted in East Asian culture and is said to simply be "air, energy, breath."

The Chakras are the seven mystical spheres of light that encircle the body, mind, and spirit.

My Reiki One class included one day of instruction at a wellness center in Harrisburg, Pennsylvania. A guided meditation, instruction manual, and an attunement were part of the offerings.

"What is an attunement?" I asked my Reiki One teacher.

"An attunement is when the already existing life force energy within you is turned on!" she said with kindness and enthusiasm. "Reiki One is all about self-healing, self-care, and getting your vibrations elevated."

"Getting my vibrations elevated?" I asked.

"Yes. As a human, it is normal and healthy to move through the spectrum of emotions in any one day, or moment. As a Reiki One student, you will learn to integrate the principles of Reiki so that you may maintain high vibrations."

Her loose-leaf chart, included in the class, showed a diagram of the vibrations and their associated emotions. The chart showed clearly why I had experienced literal vibrations the day of my Kundalini Awakening. I was starting to understand that there was so much more to learn, however I was still grateful to know that my vibrations were, in fact, *good*.

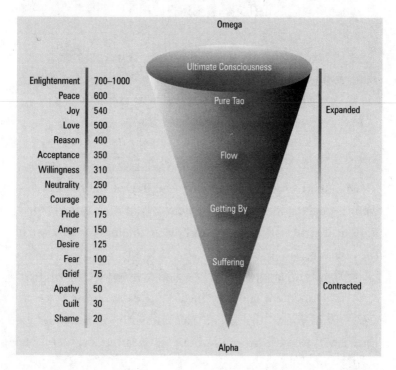

Enlightenment	700–1000	
Peace	600	
Joy	540	Expanded
Love	500	
Reason	400	
Acceptance	350	
Willingness	310	
Neutrality	250	
Courage	200	
Pride	175	
Anger	150	
Desire	125	
Fear	100	
Grief	75	
Apathy	50	Contracted
Guilt	30	
Shame	20	

I moved through the remainder of the class without too many expectations, took my Reiki manual, received my attunement, and returned home. Still, I needed to know more about what happened to me during the Kundalini Awakening. I remembered the intense sensations that began at my bottom, and I learned that those sensations correlated to my root chakra.

I began to understand that each of the seven chakras corresponds to a time during a person's development, sensations within the body, and a color that is unique to each chakra.

First chakra	The womb to 6 months	Root	Red
Second chakra	6 months to 2.5 years	Sacral	Orange
Third chakra	2.5 years to 4.5 years	Solar plexus	Yellow
Fourth chakra	4.5 years to 6.5 years	Heart	Green
Fifth chakra	6.5 years to 8.5 years	Throat	Blue
Sixth chakra	8.5 years to 14 years	Third eye	Indigo
Seventh chakra	14 years to 21 years	Crown	Violet

We know that the spirit is eternal, and that the physical body has a limited life, here on Earth. With that knowledge comes the *duality* of our human experience. Naturally, then, there are emotions that are also dualistic that correspond to the seven chakras.

First chakra	To be here	Survival	Fear
Second chakra	To feel	Sexuality	Guilt
Third chakra	To act	Power	Shame
Fourth chakra	To love	Love	Grief
Fifth chakra	To speak	Communication	Lies
Sixth chakra	To see	Intuition	Illusion
Seventh chakra	To know	Cognition	Attachment

The chakras felt like the building blocks of expression for the spirit. Similar to how letters of the alphabet have their own shape and sound but combine to create words and language, each chakra is also associated with sound and vibration.

	Sound	Mantra	Note
First chakra	LAM 396 hertz	I am safe	C
Second chakra	VAM 417 hertz	I am creative	D
Third chakra	RAM 528 hertz	I am powerful	E
Fourth chakra	YAM 639 hertz	I am loved and I am loving	F
Fifth chakra	HAM 741 hertz	I am expressive	G
Sixth chakra	OM 852 hertz	I am perceptive	A
Seventh chakra	OM 963 hertz	I am at peace	B

The etheric energy of vibration correlated to my new-found friendly words: life force energy, prana, and qi. But I also discovered that the chakras had tangible and earthly attributes, as well. They are represented in gemstones. The colors of the stones also correspond to the colors of the chakras.

First chakra	Black tourmaline, bloodstone, garnet
Second chakra	Carnelian, copper, sunstone
Third chakra	Amber, citrine, golden tiger eye
Fourth chakra	Emerald, ruby, rose quartz
Fifth chakra	Aquamarine, larimar, turquoise
Sixth chakra	Amethyst, labradorite, lapis lazuli
Seventh chakra	Amethyst, clear quartz, moonstone

The effects of the Kundalini Awakening were still lingering, even as I gathered supportive evidence and information. Maryanne had a strong sense of confidence when she offered her reading to me. She trusted the information she was given about my life implicitly, and I was amazed by how assured she was. She had never met me before and had no personal information available to her that she could have possibly Googled. In fact, my great-grandmother Anna was present during my very first reading with Maryanne—and Maryanne identified her and named her without any hesitation. Even still, I had to figure things out for myself.

For the next twenty-one days, after my Reiki attunement, I dutifully practiced the meditations and hand positions outlined in the Reiki One manual. I was awkward and uncertain at first, leaning over my book to ensure I was doing it "right," but while my son was at school and my daughters took their afternoon naps, I committed to one full hour of self-Reiki daily.

The self-Reiki proved to show signs of effectiveness. I had been plagued by eczema on my hands and wrists for years. In the past, I had seen my general practitioner physician as well as dermatologists but to no avail; the eczema always erupted—especially on my left hand under and around my wedding rings. At times, my left hand would swell so much that my wedding ring would not fit.

By the end of the first week of self-Reiki, to my surprise, the eczema disappeared. By the end of the second week, I slipped into deep meditative states as tears silently streamed from my eyes each session. Week three came with a centered peace and a grounded sense of calm. The eczema, as I discovered, was a symbol of irritations resting on the surface (that I had carried with me for far too long) and had been waiting to be released. It was the beginning of many outward expressions of healing, clearing, and change. Even now, the eczema has never returned.

Spring of 2012 was met with a new sense of enthusiasm, and I returned to the wellness center in Harrisburg for Reiki Two. This time, class was all about *sharing* life force energy. I was eager to develop a seamless practice, and after my Reiki Two attunement, I attended many Reiki Shares. Reiki Shares are typically free events where attuned practitioners meet to give Reiki and receive it for themselves. It was a good opportunity for me to seesaw between my responsibilities at home with the children and my newfound peers.

I found the spiritual community in the Harrisburg area to be supportive and progressive. There were invitations to try this modality or that technique, workshops and events, and one gem of a bookstore that invited me deeper into my self-awareness than I had ever known possible.

Jan and Paul Wren owned The Inner-Connection bookstore in New Cumberland, Pennsylvania, for over thirty years. The shop sat on the corner of a sleepy, tree-lined street just across the Susquehanna River from Harrisburg. It was neighbored by Salon Elena, with pink walls and a lovely, multilingual hairstylist, Tanya, who waved to the postman and the passersby; Villa Roma pizza shop, with a floor-to-ceiling mural of the Twin Towers and New York City skyline, serving the best "slice n' a *Coke*!" around; and Morris Laundromat, coin-operated self-service "Since 1959."

One day, after a haircut at Salon Elena, I knew my girls were still napping at home, so I stopped into the bookstore. The shopkeeper's bell rang as I entered "The IC" for the first time on a warm Saturday afternoon.

Jan greeted me as though I were her own granddaughter returning home. I was surprised by her resemblance to the actress Shirley MacLaine, and upon meeting her, realized her personality matched as well. She was as savvy in business as she was with her wit, and had me figured out by the time I turned the first set of bookshelves.

"Hello, dear. What brings you in today?" She smiled.

"I'm just browsing, thank you," I said as I eyed the glass case of angel knickknacks.

Every nook and cranny were filled with books about angels,

auras, chakras, divination, health, manifesting, mediumship, numerology, saints, spirits, and symbology. Gemstones, sage sticks, and fairy figurines filled the aisles. It was as though the shop stood still in time.

It was quiet and peaceful.

Jan lowered her glasses, eyed me up and down, and said, "Come. Follow me," and we walked toward the big bookcase in the back.

"Paul . . . PA-ul," she shouted as we approached a wall of books. "Do we have any more Louise Hay?"

"Who?" Paul asked.

"Louise. LOU-ISE," she said sharply as though Louise were a personal friend of theirs.

"Oh, Louise. Yes, of course. For Pete's sake, no need to shout, Jan. I'll get it. I'll get it."

"Who's Louise?" I asked, leaning in, hoping not to disrupt the peace.

"Oh, well dear, Louise Hay?" she said with a smile. "She just so happens to be the godmother of everything good around here. She is an author and an all-around amazing lady. Quite a story. *Quite* a story!"

Paul, opening the curtained doorway to the storage room, returned and presented me with *You Can Heal Your Life* by Louise Hay, which I promptly bought, thanked them for their suggestion, and returned home. My bedside nightstand was starting to fill up with stacks of new reading material. Louise and *You Can Heal Your Life,* however, would be a cornerstone to further my own self-healing and prompt me to earn my Reiki Master Teacher certification.

> ## When the student is ready the teacher will appear . . .
> —BUDDHA

I was practicing self-Reiki routinely and had begun practicing Reiki for just about anyone else that I could get my hands on . . . literally. But I still needed to meet with the second teacher, "the angel lady," as Maryanne referred to her: Candy Danzis. I recalled what Maryanne had said: "Go see Candy Danzis and learn everything you can about angels." And, without hesitation, I moved on to the next step.

The IC bookstore was the keystone to the spiritual community in the Harrisburg area. There, Jan and Paul hosted weekly events with various guest practitioners. Some classes were on angel cards, some were workshops on auras, others were information sessions on the chakra system. The angel lady, Candy Danzis, hosted monthly "Angel Circle" events where each guest received a brief reading from their guardian angel. So, for thirty-three dollars, I went to The Inner-Connection and attended my first Angel Circle.

Candy's Angel Circles filled The IC to the brim. Metal folding chairs sat end to end and guests young and old filed into the bookstore's center aisles to hear messages from Candy and the angels. She stood tall and polished, professional yet serene. She was a gifted speaker with the confidence of a leader that had been refined by personal experience. You'd never know it by listening to her speak, but she was fused by pressure and perseverance—like all diamonds. As I sat in the audience that evening, tucked in the corner, listening to the guest's messages, I observed Candy as she delivered her readings. I, too, saw the snapshots of information she was sharing, but did not yet know *how* to harness them closer to interpret the details in a manner that was relatable to each guest.

And how does she do it so gracefully? I wondered.

A Reiki Master Teacher class was forming for Mother's Day weekend, and I called Candy's office to learn more.

"Hi, Candy, this is Annemarie Heckert. I attended your Angel Circle at The Inner-Connection recently and I am interested in learning more about your upcoming Reiki Master class."

"Hi, Annemarie, yes. It is so good to hear from you. In fact, I have four additional students already registered. I like to keep my classes small, so we have lots of time to learn."

"That sounds wonderful, Candy. I would love to register. But I am only Reiki Two certified just last month and I am worried that I am not ready."

"Ah, I see," she said. I could feel her stand upright, and before speaking again, she paused, carefully, and gently said, "You are always ready. You always have been, Annemarie."

At that moment, the delivery of her words presented me with the permission to truly move forward. Later that month, in a class of five students at Candy's home on Chestnut Ridge Drive, she attuned me to Reiki Master Teacher, and thus began a whirlwind tutelage under Candy's wing for the next eighteen months.

Candy's home rested behind a natural screen of trees and a stone wall that ushered students down a lantern-lit driveway toward the front door. If Maryanne Wellington had been likened to a wise professor from Hogwarts, Candy's home was Hogwarts itself. The stone facade jutted out of the earth as confidently as a Scottish castle, and students were greeted at the front door by Candy's kind and handsome husband, Brian.

Inside, the walls and rooms were adorned with paintings and statues of angels. A gold statue of Archangel Michael, wings expanded and sword at the ready, stood watch from Brian's den. All of Candy's workshops were hosted in her large family room or in the sunroom that overlooked the western skyline and mountains. A gazebo draped in purple wisteria sat in the foreground and was admired by all.

"It is beautiful, isn't it? It's a fast grower, too!" Candy said with enthusiasm and pride as we praised the wisteria from her sunroom that May afternoon in 2012. I could tell Candy was not a native of Pennsylvania and in some ways, wanted to create a sanctuary that resembled parts of her past. Originally from Southern California, Candy brought sunshine, color, and radiance to everything and everyone. She'd had an educated, practical, and exceptional career in banking and finance before she began to work as a professional spiritual counselor and an "ambassador to the angels," as she put it. So, her interpretation and teachings were often mirrored after a corporate or organizational model.

I was not entirely sure I was supposed to be at Candy's home that day. Even though I had begun practicing Reiki and offering professional-level treatments to friends and family, I still struggled with where all of this was leading me. Even still, I dutifully practiced the self-Reiki and continued to study.

Several months passed and I returned many more times to Candy's home for as many classes as she offered. "Angel Alignment One" and "Angel Alignment Two" were two of her larger workshops that focused entirely on the angels, their structure of support, and the hierarchy of "God's Team" of assistants. Aunt Betty Lou flew in from Florida and joined me in learning all about the angels in both of Candy's big workshops.

Students attended Candy's workshops from all over the country. Brian, her husband, often introduced her at events, and they wore complementary outfits that kept them looking like the sharp, unified team that they were. For Angel Alignment One, our classmates seemed to be much farther along in their skill sets than me. I was so happy to have Aunt Betty Lou to discuss the content of the classes in the evenings. We often stayed up late, sharing a bottle of wine and dissecting the information we had learned. We were two eager students and took great joy in discovering everything we could about the angels from Candy.

Our classmates were giving angel card or tarot card readings already. Most were Reiki Master Teachers or well-intended healers that had day jobs while still exploring the esoteric. Some students attended Candy's workshops seeking instructions on how to connect with their own deceased family members. One mother in particular had lost a teenage son in a car accident. She dutifully sought signs and symbols to stay in contact with him. I knew I was fated to offer readings of my own, but how? And *professionally*?

In Candy's class one day, we covered an in-depth look at the seven chakras, the angels that correspond with them, and how life force energy can be utilized as a means to interpret messages from the soul. I felt like I had been given the keys to the castle! I had already started to learn about the chakras through my Reiki classes, so this was a topic I could connect with.

"The chakras," Candy said, "are like the instrument panel in your vehicle. If something needs attention, it will light up. It's truly our light body."

She suggested additional books like *The Wheels of Life* by Anodea Judith and a book that would become my very favorite, *Anatomy of the Spirit* by Caroline Myss. I read everything she suggested.

As I floated between my role as a mother and that of developing my gifts as a Medium, I returned to my first introduction to life force energy and the principles of Reiki.

The Five Principles of Reiki are:
Just for today, I will not be angry.
Just for today, I will not worry.
Just for today, I will do my work honestly.
Just for today, I will be kind to my neighbors and every living being.
Just for today, I will be thankful for all of my blessings.

Now, these principles may seem simple enough, but applying them to every moment, every thought, and every interaction can prove to be quite intense. *Good thing there's forgiveness,* I often thought. I suppose students of Reiki are offered compassion with "just for today" in their practice, so as not to become discouraged by the occasional meltdown, unpleasant remark, or reaction. After all, Rocky Balboa was right when he said, "The world ain't all sunshine and rainbows."

The third Reiki principle, "Just for today, I will do my work honestly," always stood out to me. I was certainly not a dishonest person, but I knew I was not being honest with myself. I still needed to gain experience and, most importantly, confidence in order to begin offering my gifts professionally. But, man, I just wanted to be at home with my children, Christopher, Maria, and Anna.

Becoming a good mom and having a big family had always been my only dream. That was it. That was all I ever really wished for. In retrospect, I never knew I could have dreamed a little bigger or broader to include a family *and* career. And certainly not simultaneously! I never, ever anticipated that it would be my dream of becoming a really good mom that would ultimately push me into my soul purpose work as a Medium.

AUTHENTIC

Back at my home, as I busied myself with the daily care of the children, my husband Doyle and I had become increasingly distant. An only child, he came from loving and caring parents and grew up participating in Boy Scouts, soccer, football, and skiing, so I was blindsided when Doyle's actions did not seem to follow his parents' model. Our son was the first baby he had ever held, and I tried to be patient with him as he developed a paternal instinct. From my perspective, though, Doyle struggled with the responsibility of becoming a father. Early on in our relationship, I discovered that Doyle regularly used alcohol and pornography, but he did more than I was comfortable with.

When Doyle and I first met in 2002, we lived right across town from each other. Once we moved in together and were married, I began to suspect that Doyle chose to stay home and indulge in his interests rather than working or taking care of his responsibilities. I felt confused by the way the hopes and dreams he had shared with me regarding a family contrasted with his actions. He knew that I found his interests unappealing, and I suspected that he therefore began to hide them from me. I found this pattern to feel like a betrayal, although he assured me it was still under control.

It was a very difficult time for me. Externally, we appeared as a content, loving couple whose lives together were opening up in the direction of our dreams. Internally, though, I never knew which version of Doyle I was going to be talking with—the smart, kind, music-loving man that I fell in love with, or the man that appeared to have deeply rooted secrets and hidden habits.

Leaving the children home with Doyle for a day while

I was attending a workshop left me feeling terribly anxious and divided. I was often concerned for their safety and would sometimes worry that Doyle wouldn't be able to take care of them well if he was checked out. I felt frazzled and exhausted.

The clinical counseling I had sought for my self-confidence in advance of my marriage set the groundwork for me to seek support once married. For years within the marriage I struggled with what I viewed as a betrayal of trust and intimacy from my husband, so I confided in my therapist, Raymond.

"Hi, Annemarie. Nice to see you again. How are things going today?" Raymond asked warmly as I took a seat on the lumpy sofa in his office.

Raymond's office was one of several counselors' offices situated in a historic building on the town square. His walls were painted pink, and spider plants draped over the windowsills onto bookshelves. Several diplomas hung on the wall adjacent to his desk, where dust had accumulated in the corners of the frames over the years. He wore khaki pants and brown Birkenstocks. A sign emblazoned with a rainbow stating "All are welcome here" haphazardly hung on the doorknob and reminded me of a high school bathroom pass. I loved working with Raymond. I felt safe talking to him in the pink office. He always knew the right questions to ask and the right time to ask them.

The box of tissues on the end table was routinely emptied due to my tears at the end of our hour-long sessions. I tried to make sense of what was going on behind closed doors at home but could never wrap my head around why Doyle seemed to sink deeper and deeper into his habits. Raymond and I dis-

cussed strategies to suggest to Doyle. While he could not diagnose Doyle himself, Raymond attempted to equip me with
the tools necessary to cope at home as I began to understand
what was happening.

I desperately attempted to hold on to some semblance of
health and stability in our family, but my thoughts became
entangled in Doyle's behavior. His interests made me feel like
*I'm not pretty enough. I'm too demanding, or I have become too
matronly.*

It was just after his thirty-seventh birthday that the weight
of this situation came down on me, and I needed to make a
formal decision. I had wrestled with the thought of leaving
Doyle in the past, but now, with three young children and no
career of my own, I turned back to my mentor Candy, whom
I trusted deeply, in a private, formal reading for clarity before
I made my final choice.

Candy and I sat across from each other in the upstairs office
of her home on Chestnut Ridge Drive. A circular ceiling mural
of angels in pastel blues and golds looked down upon us as we
came together, as trusted mentor and student, to reveal the potential trajectories of my future. In a serious and deliberate tone,
Candy invited in all her support angels and, with a deep breath,
shared the images and information about my choices. Candy and
the angels never made decisions for me. Instead, she illuminated
the paths that were available for *me* to choose. It was up to me to
decide. As she revealed the choices, she paused, looked me right
in the eye, and said, "And where, Annie, do you feel most at
peace? Where do you feel most *authentic*?"

She guided me to write "AUTHENTIC" on a yellow sticky

note and place it on my bathroom mirror, refrigerator, or purse—a simple strategy to keep it active in my awareness—but the lesson had already been understood. The next step was application; I needed to process my plan.

After our reading, Candy stood outside her home's front door. The cool, damp spring air blanketed my blue car. She stood confidently with both hands on her hips, watching me when she waved goodbye. I drove home in silence. I knew that no matter what, I had to go.

The next morning, I called my beloved friend Aaron from the Navy, who lived in New York. "How will I take care of Christopher, Maria, and Anna by myself? And how will I ever be able to tell people that I am a Medium? They'll look at me like I am crazy!" I said with a lump in my throat and tears in my eyes. Aaron, the ever-empathetic friend, said, "Oh, honey. It will be every day. For the rest of your life, it will be every day."

By the end of that month, I had decided to formally approach Doyle for a separation. I had hoped my request for time apart would prompt him to seek positive changes. Instead, he rented a seedy studio-style apartment right next door to a bar downtown. It was all the confirmation I needed to move forward with custody and divorce proceedings. I was devastated.

The early years with Doyle had been full of adventure, music, and laughter. I struggled deeply with discerning the right decision. I never wanted to be a single mother and I did not want to break up my family. But the pressure caused by his lifestyle became too unbearable for us to coexist together. The fear of staying together outweighed the fear of moving forward without him in my immediate life. It took me years of clinical counseling, trial and error, and patience followed by urgency to conclude that by leaving Doyle, I was in fact being honest and authentic. It was a huge revelation to me, and I carried the intentions of *honesty* and *authenticity* like a sword and shield as I moved forward.

THE CODE

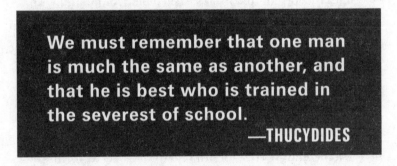

> We must remember that one man is much the same as another, and that he is best who is trained in the severest of school.
>
> —THUCYDIDES

Do you remember the movie *The Karate Kid*? I love the part specifically when the student Daniel-san confronts his teacher, Mr. Miyagi, about his training because he is feeling as though he is unprepared for the fight. Mr. Miyagi says, "Either you karate do 'yes' or karate do 'no.' You karate do 'guess so,' (get squished) just like grape."

Candy had been referring clients to me for Reiki treatments and I began to build a book of clients that would come to my home office for care. I set up a Reiki table as well as a small table and two chairs by the windows in my home office.

While performing the Reiki treatments, I would see colors that corresponded to different body parts, illnesses, and emotions. When I paused over any one color, I could see snapshots of images pertaining to the client's health. The longer I held my hands over the color, the more in-depth details I could discern. I could clairvoyantly see skin, bones, tissue, veins, and blood vessels—all the way down to the cellular level. My range of scope was unlimited, and I could see how emotions such as unreleased trauma, grief, and guilt were the hotbed of a host of illnesses.

Quickly, I began to correlate the colors around and within my client to match the chakra system that Candy had taught me. The colors of red, orange, yellow, green, pink, blue, indigo, and violet created a shining spectrum of light for me to gain information about each client. The colors were the code to the light body.

Each day, I welcomed new and returning clients to my home office. Oftentimes I noticed patterns and themes in their energetic fields. Three last week suffered from anxiety. Two this week had stored sexual abuse trauma. And one routine client, Kara, had cancer.

Kara came into my home with long, thick black hair and the petite frame of an athlete. Dressed in layers of bohemian-style clothing, she would quickly sink into a meditative state on my Reiki table. I was in treatment with Kara, with my eyes closed and focus directed to her second chakra, when I was able to see into the far corners of her hips. She had recently received treatment to remove cancerous tumors around her ovaries. I could see that the interior lining of her uterine wall was light brown and watery. As I treated the area where the cancer had been discovered with the white light of Reiki, I could see that the cells surrounding the newly vacant lining were working hard to become clear and healthy like the cells farther back into her body. I knew it would require time; consistent meditation; good foods; a positive, nurturing environment; and love to persuade the cells from duplicating in a cancerous manner again.

Aside from having multiple pregnancies, and the associated labor and deliveries, I had no formal training with biology or anatomy and lacked the language to identify precisely what I was seeing. In fact, personally I was a bit of a medical enigma. I had 20/20 vision, had never broken a bone or even had a cavity. So, the aspect of medical-related clairvoyance was, as they say in the South, "a whole 'nother thing."

One afternoon when my children were at school, I felt the temperature drop in my home office while Kara was on the Reiki table. I clairaudiently heard the voice of a deceased woman and felt her standing at Kara's crown. I listened carefully while holding steady my position over Kara's second chakra. The spirit identified herself as Kara's grandmother— "the one that had been with Kara on the day she chose her wedding dress, and it was her swimming pool where Kara had accidentally been left unattended and nearly drowned as a little girl." I sensed that her grandmother was sharing these stories for validation, and I meticulously paid attention to the details she described.

After the Reiki treatment, I asked Kara to join me at the small table I had in the office to go over the details of the treatment. She happily obliged and I shared with her the images I had seen of her now-healing second chakra and the guest appearance from her grandmother. Kara grabbed a tissue and burst into tears and confirmed that yes, her grandmother had been with her the day she purchased her dress and that yes, in fact, she had almost drowned as a small girl when her mother had rushed off to the bathroom. Her grandmother assured me that Kara had plenty of time remaining on this Earth and, like the accident at the swimming pool, she will continue to be protected by her angels through her recovery from cancer. It was a beautiful moment for both of us. I had been so happy to convey the messages and the unexpected visit from Kara's grandmother as well as the clairvoyant scan of her recovery. I don't think either one of us will ever forget that day.

I began to understand that the formula for which I would access information was being offered to me in a sacred and honorable space. The years in my childhood and young adulthood, where unbound and deeply personal information came to me by uninvited guest spirits with billboard-sized images with developmentally too mature content, had *started* to become a narrowed channel of time, energy, and focus. I was so grateful. I was beginning to understand that the Kundalini Awakening was in fact my personal wake-up call and, for the first time, I thanked God daily for my gifts.

If I could relay messages to clients in the same sacred space as I had to Kara, I would surely be doing what I believed God had intended me to do.

Lord, make me an instrument of your peace, I thought.

The Reiki clients continued to come to me, first by Candy's referral and then through word of mouth. Candy had recently given a reading to Sue, who, like Kara, was newly recovering from cancer treatment.

Sue had been riddled with grief over the potential that she would be consumed by cancer and crossover before she and her adult children could be prepared. Candy had sent Sue to me so I could alleviate her emotional distress, ground her anxiety, and clear away any worry that might still be lingering.

When Sue was on my Reiki table, however, I was shown that her body had not responded to the cancer treatment completely. And that, very quickly, Sue's lymph nodes would swell with inflammation, taking her back to her oncologist where again, she would be diagnosed with cancer. This time, the outcome looked very different than Kara's. This time, I was careful to offer precisely only the Reiki treatment, and even though Sue urged me to let her know if anything looked *off*, I erred on the side of letting her physicians diagnose her in a manner that was timely and appropriate. After all, I am not medically trained.

After Sue's treatment, though, confused as to how to have handled the information I was given, I called Candy. It was important to me to be honest, but in a responsible manner, and without frightening Sue. Candy assured me that I had handled Sue's treatment well and that in fact, Reiki and the chakras complement clinical medicine and are never meant to be a substitute. "Medicine is from God, too," she said. A breast cancer survivor herself, Candy was well aware of the importance of delivering information delicately and responsibly.

"But, Candy." I hesitated. "What do I say when I see that a client's medical treatment won't be enough? What do I tell them if I see that they won't survive?"

Candy tenderly said, "You don't. That's between your client and God—the timing. But what you can tell them is to make themselves as comfortable as possible." I jotted down her exact phrasing as I stretched the phone charger across the kitchen to my notepad. I thought, *I hope I never have to repeat that phrase to anyone.*

SURRENDER AGAIN

Aside from the growth in my work with the Reiki clients, the kids and I were getting by, barely. Over the course of the summer of 2013, with the reality of raising three children on my own, I became overwhelmed with grief. I lost over twenty pounds in a month. My hair thinned and my menstrual cycle stalled. I was devastated to know that my children would not grow having a father at home. Nor would there be any guarantee that Christopher, Maria, and Anna would remain safe in Doyle's care during his custodial time. My anxiety was at an all-time high. I was in shock and worried about every little thing. Anna was just two and still sleeping in a crib. Maria was a precocious three-year-old and still needed her beloved "binky" pacifier. And big brother Christopher, at seven years old, had to become the girls' protector when I was not with them.

I felt fragile and deeply vulnerable to the rawness of it all. None of this was how I had hoped and dreamed my big family would grow and develop. None of this was how I had intended to be as a woman, as a mother. It challenged me to my core. The thought of not seeing my three children while they were under Doyle's care terrified me. For me, there was no silence greater than that of a home without children, and on the weekends while the kids were away, silence taunted and provoked my intentions of *honesty* and *authenticity* like a schoolyard bully whispering, "Are you sure you can do it?"

I decided to cope by staying busy and making the most of my time by being focused and productive, not just with clients, but at home, too. I started to clean. From the basement up, no corner was left untouched. I found it helpful to put to good use the lessons I was learning for inner transformation and apply them to the energy of my home by eliminating anything that was not necessary or purposeful.

One late night while the children were with Doyle, I was quietly cleaning out the kitchen when I reached far into the back corner cabinet and accidentally cut myself badly on the blade of a blender that Doyle had purchased. I saw bright red blood quickly falling from my hand even before I felt the sting of the gash. Teardrops of blood fell to the floor in slow motion as I quickly grabbed a dish towel to stop the bleeding. "Son of a bitch," I whispered, holding my hand to my heart. It was all I could do to sit on the floor of the kitchen, wrapping my hand in a dish towel, and cry.

Despite my best efforts to stay busy, the cut on my hand, and the fact that there was no one there to help me, pummeled me to the floor. And I wept until the tears from my eyes and the blood from my hand ceased. I recalled what

Candy had said to me. "There's no part of this that you cannot handle." And I stood up and said out loud to God, "God! If you need me to do this work, if you *absolutely* require it of me . . . then I will do it. And I will give You everything . . . *all* . . . of my life's purpose to *You*. But I WILL NOT DO IT if my children are not safe. I will walk away from this work, and I will bury my gifts, once and for all." It was a turning point, for sure.

Later, as I washed out the blood-soaked dish towel and laid it to dry, I realized how it resembled a white flag . . . and that I had surrendered once again. As the days passed, my cut now bandaged and healing, I was still processing the events, my feelings, and my agreement to God. I personified God up in Heaven as Robin Williams's character Sean Maguire, the court-ordered therapist in *Good Will Hunting*, patiently waiting for my temper and despair to pass. I knew full well that I would approach doubt and fear again and again—however forgiving of my very messy, resistant, human process.

I remembered the vibrational frequency chart and scolded myself for being pissed off at God. *Now how, exactly, am I "enlightened"?* I thought. So, if Robin Williams's character could symbolize God, he could also uplift my spirit. So, I turned to his comedy acts to get me laughing. As devastated as I was, I could not hide anymore. If this was my plight, then I might as well make the most of it. And I needed all the humor I could get.

The income from Reiki clients provided just enough to make ends meet. The more the clients came, the more I practiced linking into the code of the chakras to read their energy. The more I read my clients' energy, the more I practiced delivering messages to them. The more messages my clients received, the more clients came. Soon, I was casually coupling my Reiki treatments with angel card readings. Then, naturally, I began to offer the two services uniquely.

Angel card readings were really very simple for me. I was already reading everyone, everywhere, all the time anyway, but like the chakra system for my Reiki clients, angel cards would be the building blocks for my clairvoyant readings. They gave me an infrastructure. As part of Candy's Angel Alignment Two class, each student received their own deck of angel cards. And man, I loved them. I would stay up late and have grand spreads of cards across my kitchen table, drinking hot chai and listening to the blues, Otis Redding, or Etta James while the kids slept. I carried my first deck of angel cards with me in my purse and happily offered off-the-cuff card readings to just about anyone that asked. It was as effortless and on time as the autumn leaves burning bright reds and golds.

Soon the accuracy of these little angel card readings began to send clients calling just for a reading. And with the extra money coming in, I gladly accepted the invitation to participate in small events at The Inner-Connection bookstore or benefits at fire halls where Mediums, tarot and rune readers, Reiki practitioners, and I each offered our services. It was such a hodgepodge of characters and backgrounds that I remember thinking *This must be what the Barnum & Bailey Circus was like.*

At my very first event, my twenty-minute angel card readings were sold out within forty-eight hours of being advertised.

The day of the event, my babysitter was running late and I raced out the door to arrive on time—only to forget my deck of angel cards at home. I realized what was happening. Just like all the pushes from my angels in the past, this was the fateful nudge I needed to once and for all offer clairvoyant readings.

I was the rookie reader that day; even in circuses such as this, there was still a hierarchy of intuitives. The little room where I met with my clients was in the far back, squeezed down a narrow, creaky-floored hall, where a small table was wedged between a photocopier and a sink. I thought, *Well, Annie . . . what the hell?* and gave 100 percent of my attention to each client and their guardian angels that sat with me that day. I gave it my all.

When the first few clients' readings were complete, I would sit silently, waiting, eyes squinched closed, praying—half expecting them to march straight to the front desk and ask for their money back. Instead, rather—and quite to my surprise—I heard hushed affirmations of accuracy and relevance as they passed the next client in line. So . . . I just kept going and gave every ounce of focus that I had to my clients. I knew firsthand just how important receiving messages could be.

That evening, exhausted, I returned home with just enough money to pay the babysitter, and fifteen dollars to spare. *How am I supposed to keep this up?* I thought. *This is no way to support a family.* So, later that night with tear-filled eyes, as I stood at the kitchen sink washing the day's dishes, I said out loud to my angels and God again, "If this is what I am supposed to be doing then you have got to help me. I cannot support three children on fifteen dollars. I need to feel safe."

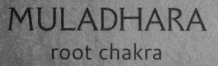

MULADHARA
root chakra

1

THE ROOT CHAKRA

The next morning, before 9:00 A.M., the phone rang.

"Hello, Annemarie?" she asked.

"Yes, hello, this is Annemarie."

"Annemarie, this is Johanna Erdmann. You gave me a reading yesterday afternoon."

"Yes," I said, holding my breath nervously. I was certain she had called to scold me or to tell me how incredibly off my reading was.

"I just want to thank you so much for all that you have done for me. The reading you gave me yesterday brought me so much peace."

"Oh! Oh, wow! Thank you, Johanna! I am so happy to hear this."

"Annemarie, how much do you charge for a full hour session? I would like to schedule one with you right away."

At this point in time, I had no business model set up. I blurted out, "One hundred dollars for a one-hour reading."

"Great," Johanna replied. "I'll take three."

And with that, I fumbled for a pen, stuttering over my

words as she shared her availability and made arrangements for her readings.

My prayers had been answered, and I thanked God and the angels right out loud.

On the days that the children were in school or with their dad, I spent every single minute working or studying. I was constantly refining my readings and learning more about energy.

I often thought, *damn. If I could just find a course on* How to Be a Medium: 101, *I would take it.* But, sure enough, each time I reached a plateau, a new book would come to me—and always in the most unusual of ways. My friend Liz's hunky massage therapist, who moonlighted as a bartender, suggested I read *Eastern Body, Western Mind: Psychology and the Chakra System as a Path to the Self* by Anodea Judith.

Despite my challenges with academics, books have always been like friends to me. I read Anodea's work and was so impressed by the detail and the delivery. The feeling that I had known the material all before arose again, and with each chapter, I felt increasingly confident that I was learning something instrumental to my calling. It felt like meeting a soulmate— you know. You had only known them for a minute, but you felt like you had known them forever. I was so grateful for her work as it propelled me toward greater confidence.

Anodea defines the chakra system as a "human biocomputer" where "the word chakra literally means disk." She goes on to compare the chakra system to that of a computer, including a hard drive and software. She states,

"In this analogy the body is the hard drive, our programming is the software, and the Self is the user. However, we did not write all of these programs, and some of their language is so archaic it is unintelligible. It is a heroic challenge, indeed, to identify our programs and rewrite them all while continuing to live our lives, yet this is the task of healing."

This is the task of healing, I thought, recalling the Spruce Street mystic's message: "You must first heal yourself." It felt like this was a landmark pointing me in the direction of personal peace and well-being. Heaven knows that is what my soul was seeking as my divorce proceedings lingered on and new clients continued to call. This incredible resource would become my go-to for deciphering the chakra system. In effect, this knowledge led to a sense of trust in the delivery of my readings and so much more.

The first step, I think, is to understand that the chakras are a metric to describe the architecture of the spirit, or light body. There are seven primary chakras and each one builds upon the other to create a network of concentric circles in and around the framework of the human body. Each circle contains a matrix of spokes connected by energy, thereby creating a wheel of light. This very wheel of light was how I began to interpret the patterns in my readings with my clients. Clients like Johanna Erdmann.

I met Johanna again for her one-hour reading at my home, where I invited her to sit with me at my kitchen table. She came into my home rather quietly, however kindly, and sat patiently as I collected my notepaper and pen. The reading we'd had together at the recent event was a twenty-minute-long brief snapshot into a much larger moving picture. I began my second reading with Johanna as I do every reading, with a short prayer invoking my guardian angels for protection and her guardian angels for information. Aside from our twenty-minute session, I had never met Johanna, and knew nothing about her past. I did not even know how to correctly spell her last name (which was a name through a previous marriage of hers).

While I trusted my guardian angels to guide good clients to me and my home, they were still complete strangers to me.

To my surprise, a young man in spirit entered the room and stood behind me on my right. He was a teenager on the brink of adulthood, wearing a blue hooded sweatshirt and oversized khaki pants. He showed me that he carried a lighter in his pants pocket and had a loving, kind, and humble heart. There was no mistaking him; it was Johanna's son. He had been the jewel of her heart and a happy-go-lucky teenager when he was introduced to prescription pain pills by a high-school peer. As the images revealed themselves to me, I saw a movielike sequence of scenes that I narrated to Johanna. Without a sound, she nodded.

Connor was the youngest of Johanna's three children and came to me seeking solace. She *knew* he was now safe "at home" in Heaven, but she missed his presence on Earth. Remember the two additional readings she called to schedule? They were for Connor's siblings, now in college and grieving the loss of their brother in their own ways.

Johanna's and her family's loss of Connor created a ripple effect within their lives and their trajectories. No one in the Erdmann family took anything for granted, and they seemed to make their movements forward through a lens of deep appreciation for what was and a sincere hope for what will come when they are all reunited again in Heaven. As I peered down the path for what is to come for them, it was as though their entire family tree had been struck by lightning, with wounded branches and splintered bark now exposed to the elements. In time, the loss of Connor would safely be sealed into their hearts, but for now, tremors of the shock remained.

The root chakra is the very foundation for what we know to be. In our physical body, it begins at our coccyx and stretches south through our legs, feet, and toes, connecting us to the earth. In our spiritual body, the root chakra energetically grounds us, helping us to feel "charged" with excitement by exercise like walking or running. The root chakra laces together the physical and the spiritual.

In our emotional body, the root chakra is how we sense safety and connectedness. It is where we claim to be, and where we identify ourselves as part of a tribe or family unit. It is our physical and emotional stillness that precedes first steps. It is also in the stillness that we connect to our spiritual support team—such as angels and ancestors.

When I was in session with Johanna, I saw that her perception of safety had been completely compromised by the trauma and shock of her son's abrupt crossing. She was raw and vulnerable, but her guardian angels guided me to illustrate the importance of Johanna's sense of compassion as she began the grief process, her sense of groundedness and safety. She would remain safe on the Earth, and stillness and self-care would be her way of bringing her attention to the present moment.

CLUSTERS

Over the next few weeks, I noticed a pattern in the clients that were coming to me: they were all struggling with root chakra challenges. As hungry as I was for more information and more signs from the Universe regarding my own well-being, I began to listen carefully to the messages that guardian angels and deceased family members were offering to my clients as not just guidance for them—but for me, too. After all, I was the perfect candidate for root chakra stabilization. The structure of my immediate family had completely changed, my sense of safety had therefore been compromised, and I was still uncertain as to how to move forward.

The very techniques I was guided to introduce to my clients, I now began to apply to myself. At first, they felt unusual, and I questioned if I was utilizing my limited free time wisely, but I quickly discovered the benefits of routine Reiki treatments for the purpose of grounding, along with quiet time, good foods, and exercise. I felt naturally compelled to let go of consuming almost all animal products: dairy and meats. I had been an active, athletic person before meeting Doyle, and I took a lot of joy in running again. And, as simple as it sounds, I took Epsom salt baths to clear my energy and ground a little more. I found that I could quickly dip into deep meditation, where, for the first time in a very long time, I could *be* in my body and feel safe.

The root chakra teaches us that our body is the temple of the soul. It is not *out there* in some illustrious abstract external source. Our body houses all that our soul needs in order to feel centered and complete. The more we can integrate into our body, the more we can feel safe. The safer we feel, the more apt we are to take steps forward.

My observations of how we can first identify that our earthly challenges are a result of chakra imbalances go even further. Some clients have roots so deeply programmed that they do not immediately respond to the suggestions of their spiritual support. Instead, they dig in, and attempt to shut out, shut down, or outdo their intuitive guidance, creating an exhaustive process that inevitably results in surrender. Sound familiar? It did to me.

I began to see my relationships like reflections of what I had been overlooking, rejecting, or running from. And oh my, it was like opening Pandora's box when I began to analyze my family's generational traumas through the lens of the root chakra. Survival steeped in great themes of sickness and grief, marked by gender bias, perpetuated unhealthy patterns in my family's line. By the time I was in discussions with my own parents about my decision to divorce Doyle, I had begun to unravel the programming passed down to me by the past. I turned to the lives of my grandmothers, Kate and Rita, to investigate further.

My paternal grandmother, Kate, was a first-generation American. Her parents had immigrated from a small Hungarian town on the border of Austria called Sopron. My great-grandparents, Josef and Katharina, came through New York's Ellis Island and settled in central Pennsylvania, where they raised their family of five children in the East End neighborhood of Steelton, Pennsylvania. The East End was truly a melting pot of many immigrant families from Italy, Germany, and Eastern Europe. During the Spanish flu of 1918, Joe and Katharina sought refuge away from the close quarters of Steelton by biding their time in the countryside north of Harrisburg. Kate's parents did not speak a lot of English, and by the time she was school age, she was often the translator for them. She became an excellent storyteller and later, as an adult, would often speak about her early childhood—walking to and from school and watching the men, with their metal lunch boxes in hand, walking to and from the town's primary employer, the steel mill. Her father, Joe, had been trained as a butcher in Hungary and continued his work in Steelton, so her family "never went without food." Some of my fondest memories of my grandmother Kate were of listening to her sing, in that graveling voice, the "old country" Austro-Hungarian songs. She taught me all the bad words, too, and sometimes my sister Jenny and I are still surprised by the insults she could make. It was absolutely criminal to be the slightest bit overweight or "sleepin' around," she'd say. She never drove a car, and relied on friends and neighbors to take her everywhere. By the time Jenny and I could drive, we had been designated as her errand runners. At the time, I begrudgingly showed up on Saturday mornings to take her to the grocery store or post office. I would often arrive a few minutes late and she'd greet me with, "Where the hell have you been?" If I was seeking compassion and gentleness, I quickly learned I would not be receiving it from her. She was notoriously sharp-mouthed, and if there was anything that I learned from her, it was to have thick skin.

While tough, Kate was frugal for herself but generous

toward her grandchildren. Although she did not have much, what she did have, she gave to us. She showed me how to be conservative, how to make a meal last, and how to laugh in the bleakest of times. When Jenny and I asked about the stacks of canned food lining the steps to her attic, she would reply, "Just in case." She would shop at yard sales for clothing, rarely buy name-brand groceries, and reuse tinfoil. For my birthday each year, without fail, she would send a handwritten card with a crisp twenty-dollar bill. The card would say, *Dear Annie, Happy Birthday! Give 'em hell!* My siblings and I had never known the degree of poverty she and her immigrant parents endured, but we saw how the effects influenced her years and years later.

My maternal grandmother, Rita, was a second-generation American born to Frank and Anna Lafferty—both sets of families had immigrated from Ireland (County Cork, Ireland, and County Antrim, North Ireland) as a result of the effects of the potato famine. Frank and Anna established a beautiful farm in the rolling hills of Chester County, Pennsylvania, and began raising eight children of their own. As a small child, their daughter, Rita (my grandmother) came down with tuberculosis and was quarantined at home. As a result, she was held back a year from school. At age six, she and her siblings were orphaned when their mother, Anna, died in labor. Both Anna and the newborn baby died, and it was not long after that Frank, overcome by grief, fell to alcoholism and died soon after. The eight children were sent to live with Frank's sister, Sade, who raised them right along with her own children. Decades later, I asked my grandmother Rita how she ever recovered from the loss of her mother. She said, "Well, we didn't really. If one of us would cry, then we'd all cry, and Aunt Sade would have fifteen children all cryin' and that just wasn't allowed. So, we got by."

Rita recalled her mother as beautiful, loving, and kind. She never looked back on her quarantine at home with much regret, though—she viewed it as an opportunity to have stayed with "Mother a little longer." It was during her time at home that she learned how to wash clothes, change linens, and feed and take care of her baby brother, Phillip. Anna's last words to Rita were, "Take care of your baby brother," and she did. In fact, Rita eventually went on to marry, have a farmhouse, and have eight children of her own.

An excellent storyteller in her own right, Rita modeled resiliency and positivity. She was always going here or there. Throughout her life I never saw her sit down. She consistently asked me, "And now, Anniemarie, what are you learning now?" She valued education, music, the arts, travel, and dancing. To look at her as a mature woman, you would have never guessed that there was no heat in her childhood home or that she shared a bed with four of her siblings. She chose to live with courage and integrity, and her faith in God propelled her in all directions. If there was anything I learned from my grandmother Rita, it was to keep moving forward and that "through God, all things are possible."

Understanding my family's legacy was just the tip of the iceberg for me as I uncovered one layer after another of hardships. Trauma, understood, can be the source of great emotional wisdom. It demands that we adjust, regroup, and become aware.

You could find yourself feeling defeated over any one of my grandmothers' stories, really, but instead knowing that each generation comes upon their own set of challenges somehow instilled a sense of purpose in me. So, I took the best of both of my grandmothers, put it together, and decided for myself—it was time I move forward with a little luck, God, and chutzpah!

By understanding the history of my grandmothers' lives and choices, I began to understand what motivated my parents a little more. In turn, I began to see how I could influence the trajectory for myself and ultimately, for Christopher, Maria, and Anna. I knew I had to do more to get stabilized. I knew I had the power to change in me. And I knew I could not tolerate the kind of energy that I was feeling from Doyle. Moving forward looked a lot like courage but felt a lot like fear. I had to choose, every day, and sometimes hour by hour, what would it be for me? What would it be for the kids? Fear or love.

As tenacious as my grandmothers were here on the Earth, I knew that they were with me in spirit, guiding my decisions and helping me with the children. Now that Kate and Rita were in Heaven, they were no longer limited by their physical bodies and could assist me in ways that they could not have possibly done before. I began to count on them for support and I started to pay attention to the signs.

AS ABOVE, SO BELOW

Soon, I discovered that even deceased family members that my client had never met could step into readings. There are often fragmented families, unique biological lines, adoptions, and otherwise nontraditional families in Heaven and on Earth. I realized that who we call family on Earth is not always who sees us as family from Heaven. Those that watch over us from spirit do not always have an obligation to us by birth or marriage. And sometimes, they are just as involved in our day-to-day decisions as typical family members would be if they were here in the physical realm—and sometimes, even more so now that they are in spirit.

Sandra Stone first came to work with me filled with questions. With her sun-soaked blonde hair and steely, sporty figure, she looked more like a marathon runner than the United States Marine and middle school science teacher that she was. She carried a periodic table on her telephone and looked up from her spreadsheet of questions with hope in her eyes. Not long ago, she remarried, and she and her only son, Matthew, happily blended their family with Bob and his daughters, Carrie and Chelsea. Within eighteen months of marriage, Carrie and Chelsea's biological mother, Christine, crossed over after an abrupt battle with cancer. Then, without any warning, Sandra's son, fifteen-year-old Matthew, took his own life. It was a completely devastating amount of grief that brought the entire family to ask one resounding question: "Why?"

Through our sessions, I was able to go back in time, to see that Sandra and Christine had already created a soul contract to love, support, honor, and respect each other as mothers. Their bond was several lifetimes old and, together this lifetime, they had agreed to take on the theme of courage and grief.

Sandra took on the role of courage by having to experience the depth of loss of her only son. Furthermore, she took on the degree of courage necessary to experience this painful loss, and to not lose faith entirely, but instead to build new thought systems around religion and spirituality. Sandra was challenged to expand her conscious awareness beyond earthly paradigms. She was really being called to set forth on the path of the warrior: this time of spirit. This extreme test was one of endurance and patience, allowing her pragmatic scientific mind to be still, while her intuition began to slowly bloom.

Meanwhile, her stepdaughters, Carrie and Chelsea, were mourning the loss of their mother and turned to Sandra for guidance and support. I offered the family a series of readings, and in each session, we uncovered more details as to why Matthew and Christine crossed over so abruptly and within months of each other.

The readings with the Stone family pushed my limits of what I thought was possible for any one family to endure. Furthermore, after Matthew's crossing, I was absolutely overwhelmed at the level to which Sandra devoted her every moment to the study of spirituality. The Marine and long-distance runner in her made way for a kind of fortitude of hope that I had not yet seen in a client. She took to learning about the afterlife, signs from Matthew, and her guardian angels without hesitation. Sandra soon sought a PhD in theology and became a minister in a very popular Christian community. She and her husband committed their time to the ministry of God. They carry Matthew's love with them everywhere—even to remote destinations around the world to offer missionary teachings.

In one very special reading together, I saw the spirit of

Christine stand together with Matthew, hand in hand, and promise to be by Matthew's side until the time was right for Sandra and Matthew to be reunited again. Likewise, Sandra agreed to keep a steadfast watch over Carrie and Chelsea while they remained together on the Earth.

As Sandra stepped into her new path, her stepdaughters Carrie and Chelsea remained in step by returning to school to pursue additional coursework; both as healers in medicine. I was astounded by the ripple effect of inspiration that Matthew and Christine's lives had offered.

As a family, through their commitment to each other, they were all learning new and creative ways to proceed through grief and life together, on Earth and in Heaven.

ON-THE-JOB TRAINING

The clusters of clients continued throughout the remainder of 2013. In fact, not only did they build in consistency, but in quantity. With every client that walked through my door, I enlisted the support of my own guardian angels and ancestors to lift me up and validate the content of the readings. Any inkling of doubt that remained I became fastidiously aware of, and continued to lean on my angels and my guides for support. Signs, symbols, and synchronicities seemed to jump out at me, and I was grateful to make the connections so I could continue building confidence in my readings. I still felt that I was just scratching the surface for my clients. There was still so much more to learn.

I realized that the more grounded I was, the more information I could receive and the less doubt I harbored. The more information I could receive, the deeper I could go into the context of my client's story. Information was no longer paparazzi-style flashes of images around a person. The images had started to connect for every client, just like a movie. So, I continued to explore additional modalities of healing, for myself. *Makes sense, right? You can't expect to hold a lightning bolt in a mason jar, can you?* I had to expand.

It was at this time that I discovered the book *A Return to Love*, a commentary by author Marianne Williamson on a channeled book called *A Course in Miracles*. I held Marianne's words close to my heart as I moved forward with my work. She says,

"Our deepest fear is not that we are inadequate. Our deepest fear is that we are powerful beyond measure. It is our light, not our darkness that most frightens us. We ask ourselves, 'Who am I to be brilliant, gorgeous, talented, fabulous?' Actually, who are you not to be? You are a child of God. Your playing small does not serve the world. There is nothing enlightened about shrinking so that other people won't feel insecure around you. We are all meant to shine, as children do. We were born to make manifest the glory of God that is within us. It's not just in some of us; it's in everyone. And as we let our own light shine, we unconsciously give other people permission to do the same. As we are liberated from our own fear, our presence automatically liberates others."

My deepest fears—and there were a lot of them—looked a lot like cynics or naysayers standing on edge ready to pounce on any unsuspecting healer or believer. "God is Dead!" they'd shout in my imagination. Any clairvoyant grapples with the intense plague of doubt and fear until one day, doubt and fear take a back seat to the ever-evolving journey. Even now, these emotions are still present, but my litmus test for love and courage has grown stronger. Much stronger—because of the consistent reinforcement from my angels.

It is a good thing, too. By the fall of 2013, I was introduced to yin yoga, and after just one class, I registered for a two-hundred-hour yoga teacher training. I had no intention of teaching yoga, but I knew I had to develop a stronger base for myself and my body. I was still quite emotionally wobbly, and without a strong grounding routine, I felt easily tossed around—like a life raft on the ocean.

Yoga built upon my discoveries of the root chakra, gave me the words to identify the sensations I was already experiencing, and encouraged me to *stay in my body*. We studied core truths that I seemed to understand easily and, upon studying, unfolded with grace for me. After all of the years struggling with mathematics or science, this too came as a relief. I did not realize it at the time, but the Universe was preparing me, yet again, for another layer of intuition that required me to carefully detect even the slightest energetic subtlety in my body.

The term "empath" is commonly used to describe someone that has a particularly accurate barometer for another's emotions. You will hear them say, "I just *feel* what they are feeling." Sometimes, an empath may have a challenging time discerning between their own emotions and the emotions of their friend. In fact, empaths often seek coping methods to create buffers between their own emotions and others'.

Pretend an empath is wearing a white shirt. Remember Charlie Brown's friend Pig-Pen? He carried dirt and dust with him everywhere! And everywhere he went, the dirt and dust fell on everyone around him. Now, imagine wearing a white shirt and standing next to Pig-Pen. Naturally, the dirt and dust would fall onto you, and you would depart Pig-Pen's presence with some of him resting on your immaculate shirt.

Now, imagine you, the empath in the white shirt, are standing in a room full of ten Pig-Pens! The dirt and dust could become a bit anxiety inducing and overwhelming to you. Whose dirt and dust belong to whom? *Yikes.*

Clairsentience is a bit like being an empath. But instead of the exterior dust, you precisely feel the interior sensations of another human. I did my best, for years, to dull the sharp sensations of others. *She has a headache, but not a bad headache. Just dehydrated. He had an operation on his back and the pain medication has worn away today. She doesn't know it yet but will develop breast cancer and cross over in her mid-sixties. He is pre-diabetic but won't ask for help.* The list goes on and on.

Between the children, household responsibilities, and new clients, 2013 rolled quickly into 2014, and with just as much fervor as ever. By the spring of 2014, and two hundred hours of yoga later, I had gained a new ability to listen to the inner workings of not just the people around me, but this time, myself. It was a good thing, too, because clients were starting to pour in from farther away, driving to my home office from New York, New Jersey, even Florida. I was still fine-tuning the difference between the sensations of others and my own, but I could tune in or tune out easier than ever before, like the dial on a radio.

These new tools came in handy, and as quickly as I could develop a sense of confidence with one cluster of clients, I was jolted into another by an entirely new set of clients.

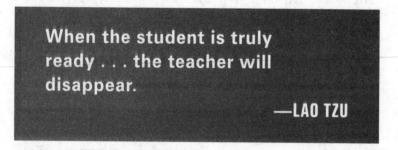

When the student is truly ready . . . the teacher will disappear.

—LAO TZU

It was an unseasonably chilly morning when Candy called me. This time, she wanted to schedule a Reiki treatment for herself. I felt honored, and fit her into the schedule the following morning.

When Candy arrived, she made no mention of any worries, and rested easily into the Reiki treatment. I had never given her Reiki before and was particularly careful to follow every step she taught me as I began at her crown chakra, where I opened her energetic pathways, and proceeded down the left side of her body, moving through her heart, solar plexus, sacral, and root chakras. I paused at her feet, placing one hand on each foot, and noticed a dramatic difference between the left and right sides of her physical body. I continued to administer the Reiki and moved up the right side of her body through the chakras, pausing again at her crown. There, I noted again the stark contrast between the sides of her body. I listened for guidance from her guardian angels.

Previously, she had briefly shared with me that she had overcome breast cancer. But it was not something that she went into expansive detail about. In fact, I felt as though it was a topic that was best left in the past and, quite frankly, as her student, none of my business.

But still, in the context of her Reiki treatment, I was called to clairvoyantly scan her body to define the imbalance. I saw that her crown appeared "glitchy," and that in time, the light would begin to blink, like a faulty light bulb, until it would burn out. I interpreted this to mean her cancer had returned.

When the Reiki treatment was complete, we sat together around the small table in my home office. "Candy," I said, searching for the words, "there's a great imbalance in your energetic fields. From left to right—not in any one chakra. It begins in your brain, and I feel as though your cancer could be returning."

I urged Candy to return to her oncologist. "Yes. I have an appointment next week," she said.

"Candy, I have never seen anything quite like this. The entire left side of your body is lacking life force energy."

With that, I noted that she was piecing together her private medical history with my assessment. She said, putting her trust into me, "If I go back to the oncologist, and they confirm our suspicions, what will the trajectory look like, Annie?" And before I could catch my words, they spilled out of my mouth and I replied, "Candy, I am afraid that it will be time to make yourself comfortable."

We looked at each other without saying another word.

The following week, Candy suffered a stroke and was rushed to the hospital. There, they discovered her cancer had in fact returned: this time in the brain.

I paused with great hesitation in knowing what might come. The mountains south of Harrisburg part just after getting into Maryland, and I took a drive there to clear my mind. I headed to the National Shrine Grotto at Mount Saint Mary's University in Emmitsburg to collect holy water to give to Candy. The Shrine Grotto was one of her favorite places, where she, too, would go to seek solace. I collected a gallon, walked along the winding paths, and sat on the bench under the canopy of summer's green leaves. The air was thick and damp by the grotto and the blue and purple hydrangeas that surrounded me brought me comfort as I sat on a bench to pray. I prayed that she would choose to stay on the Earth a little longer. Our time together had been so short.

I never got to give the holy water to Candy. God had called her home. On July 20, 2014, my mentor and confidante crossed over and returned home to Heaven. When her husband, Brian, called to tell me the news, I sat on the bottom step of the stairs and cried.

The summer of 2014 slowed to a halt. I replayed the conversations with Candy over and over again in my mind. I wanted to hold on to her wisdom and compassion as long as I could. I knew that something was happening, though, and I waited for the signs to align.

A few weeks later, as the children returned to school, I stopped by The Inner-Connection to see Jan.

"Annemarie, it is so good to see you. I am so happy you have come in today. I have been thinking about you. You know . . . you were Candy's protégé. Aside from Brian and their son, Michael, her greatest loves were the angels. And you know, nothing would make her happier than to see her work continue."

"Yes, thank you, Jan. I miss her presence so much."

"Well, I think you're ready."

"Ready?"

"Yes. Before Candy crossed over, she instructed me to ensure that you took over her Angel Circles. Now, when do you want to start?"

"Oh, wow . . . Really? I don't know if I am ready for all of that, Jan. I mean . . ."

"Now, now. Candy gave me explicit instructions, and we all know that Candy was never wrong," she said, smiling.

"It's true," I agreed. "She was never wrong."

And with that, Jan placed my name as the host of the monthly Angel Circles at The Inner-Connection.

SVADHISHTHANA
sacral chakra

2

THE SACRAL CHAKRA

The sacral chakra rests between the hips in the human body. In Sanskrit, it is referred to as "Svadhisthana" or "one's own place." It is the sacred space of creation and creativity, expansion and contraction, and is likened to a gateway where the outer world comes in. The second chakra is where our emotions are stored and the duality of such exists; anger versus compassion, dullness versus vitality, pleasure versus denial.

When in balance, the second chakra allows for a graceful flow of healthy emotions, boundaries, and an intrinsic expression of creative pursuits. When out of balance, the second chakra seeks external solutions to satisfy strong emotions. Deficiencies in the second chakra typically induce addictions—especially those involving sex.

When I first met Marco and Melissa, they were a hardworking, loyal couple that had successfully raised two children while maintaining two careers. In our work together, I was shown that Marco and Melissa had been in many lifetimes together. One lifetime, Marco had taken a vow of chastity and committed his life as a priest. In that same lifetime, he had been a close friend to Melissa, who had also taken a vow of chastity in a commitment as a nun and teacher. While this information may not seem to be entirely relevant to the trajectory of their lives, we were able to uncover several reasons for the challenges they had faced together, this lifetime, in their marriage.

In this lifetime, Marco had been an active young boy and enjoyed participating in sports and Boy Scouts in Pennsylvania. While on a Scout trip, he witnessed a camp leader sexually abusing another scout. It was terrifying for Marco, and he never returned to Scouts. For fear of any consequence, he never mentioned the abuse to his parents so as not to upset them.

Melissa came from a busy household and was often left to be babysat by her maternal uncle. Unbeknownst to her mother, Melissa was groomed and sexually assaulted by her uncle from the time she was ten.

Like Marco's, Melissa's first introduction to sex was one of abuse, a misuse of power by an authoritative person, and manipulation. While the characters were different, both stories resulted in the same trauma. A trauma that would haunt them both for their entire lives.

I was humbled to offer Marco and Melissa messages from their guardian angels on the matter of abuse to their second chakras. I was able to see that, this lifetime, they had agreed to untangle an old, antiquated limiting belief still resting in their energy around power, sex, and autonomy. And with that, while honorable, I discovered that we do not have to be an ascetic, live in an abbey, or keep contracts that bind us to any lifestyle that we have outgrown.

Through my readings with Marco and Melissa, we identified that creating new energetic pathways would benefit their healing. It was time to allow for creativity in their lives. This creativity would release the past and make room for the present. For the first time in their lives, they were given permission to create the intimacy that resonated with them. They chose to move forward in unique ways; Marco seeking healing through Reiki and exercise while Melissa sought healing through financial independence and prayer. Unlocking their soul agreements for this lifetime completely changed the way they perceived their choices regarding sex. Now, from a place of knowledge and empowerment, they are moving forward in a healthy and balanced manner.

I knew that Marco and Melissa's story was not entirely unique. As I gained more and more clients, I began to suspect that more people have experienced sexual abuse themselves, or by witnessing it, than are accounted for. In fact, my observations are that three out of four adults could claim trauma to the sacral chakra as part of their story. Offenses to the second chakra can destroy our sense of safety and are the foundations to shame that cause stagnation of our innate power within our third chakra. Abuse to the second chakra does not mean that recovery is not possible, however. Through identifying the cause, bringing it to light, and seeking forgiveness, healing is possible.

I often thought about Doyle's habits and interests, and I wondered what might have led him down that path. Today, I still work carefully and mindfully to address the deficiencies in my own second chakra that would have attracted Doyle's excessive second chakra to begin with. It is a process I continue to uncover.

> ## For Sale: Baby shoes, never worn.
> ### —ATTRIBUTED TO ERNEST HEMINGWAY

On any given day, I had several different jobs. As Mother: chauffeur, chef, cleaner, coach, nurse, nurturer, tutor; and as Medium: administrative assistant, clairvoyant, practitioner, teacher, and, mostly, student. Each and every day, I was learning. Learning how to be a better mother and learning from the spiritual support and guardian angels that stepped into my readings by what happens in the context of readings for my clients. There was never a message that I received for my client that was not in some way relevant to my own healing.

Barbara came into my home by way of referral from her son. She had just lost her husband and sought an affirmation that he had "made it" home to Heaven. She was a reserved woman, and quietly pulled her chair back from my kitchen table so as not to scuff the floor. Her white blouse had been starched and pressed crisp and her nails were painted a pale pink. The spirit of her departed spouse, George, stepped into the reading without hesitation, and right next to him stood a guardian angel carrying a small, delicately bundled newborn baby. The sweet smell of baby powder filled the room, and I acknowledged that George was, in fact, at home in Heaven with the angels and a beautiful baby girl.

Barbara was speechless as I offered details about their marriage, their two sons on the Earth, and his gratitude to Barbara for having taken care of him all the way "to the end," he said.

George went on to say, "It's okay, Barbara. The baby and I are together, and she is okay." To my surprise, Barbara began to cry, and whispered, "No one ever knew, Annemarie. No one. Not one soul. George and I never told anyone."

I clairvoyantly looked back in time and discovered that George and Barbara had been married for over forty years but had conceived a baby girl before they were wed. Immediately upon discovering she was pregnant, Barbara chose to abort the baby so as not to bring shame and embarrassment to George or their families. It was a terribly difficult decision for her, and for over forty years she had carried the weight of tremendous guilt. She feared for the soul of the baby and prayed and prayed that one day they could be reunited. She and George had committed their lives to each other, their children on Earth, and their church community. For decades, Barbara had worked toward forgiveness of herself, but could not bring herself to do so. When her husband George and a guardian angel stepped forward in the reading with such valuable information, Barbara was faced with the freedom of forgiveness. She was beyond relieved to know that the soul of her baby girl was safe in Heaven and that the love for her had never changed. Oh, and George was good, too.

Barbara was just the first woman that I witnessed struggling with how to cope with this choice. She was just one of thousands that I have offered readings to that had experienced a challenge or trauma to the second chakra. Mature women, young women, girls. Had she made the right decision? Was the soul of their baby safe in Heaven? Would they be reunited again?

I observed as her reading unfolded, and I remember thinking how important it would be for the world to know this. *Why does the world not know this?* I thought. I saw firsthand that her baby was loved and encircled with light. As a woman, as a mother, how could I not urgently offer this lesson to others like Barbara?

For me, Barbara's reading was an inspiration to more fully understand the complexities of the chakra system. I felt that I had been prepared for this work but still I had so much more to learn. I continued to study the second chakra and how the seeds of shame root into our every choice. Shame is a terrible limitation. Once brought into our lives, decisions are made around it and over it, like invasive vines at the base of a tree. The tree still grows, but the vines fight for light, eventually choking the tree of its fullest potential. Shame rests in our second chakra and affects our self-esteem.

Brené Brown, author and researcher, defines shame as "the intensely painful feeling or experience of believing that we are flawed and therefore unworthy of love and belonging—something we've experienced, done, or failed to do makes us unworthy of connection. I don't believe shame is helpful or productive."

The purpose of the second chakra is one that, in a healthy space, allows for creativity, creation, trust, attachment, and separation. I reflected back to 2008, when I had been working diligently with my therapist to move through a second chakra trauma of my own: a miscarriage. In the privacy of his office, I spoke about the need for a word to express my grief. Our son, Christopher, was three years old at the time and I wanted to expand our family before much longer. The loss of my second pregnancy ushered doubt and fear into my life like I had not yet known. I had always been very athletic, and, I thought, in tune with my body. But now, I doubted. *Will I even be able to conceive again?* I wondered.

Like Barbara, I discovered that there is a kind of grief just for dreams that do not come true. And for so many women, the babies that are not brought to fruition—through the roller coaster of unsuccessful attempts at IVF; the abortions due to emergencies, the wrong time, the wrong partner, abuse or trauma; and the miscarriages—leave women around the world asking, "Why?"

Loss, like love, has a myriad of facets—none of which are adequately identified in Western language. One constant amongst my observations for these clients is that under any one of these circumstances, each and every woman grieved the loss of the child. Across the board. Some may have moved forward with their lives faster than others, but without any hesitation, I can affirm that there is pause and there is prayer and that the souls of children that do not come to fruition are safe in the arms of the angels in Heaven.

> Your children are not your children. They are the sons and daughters of life's longing for itself. They come through you, but not of you. And though they are with you yet, they belong not to you.
>
> —KAHLIL GIBRAN

Occasionally, a client comes to me that is seeking understanding regarding energetic discord in more than one chakra. I am not surprised to find that the second chakra, the seat of intimacy and creation, often correlates to the heart chakra. The concentric circles of light in the chakras are not singularly in motion. Like the inner workings of an old-fashioned clock, one wheel turns the other. In the case of my client Gemma and her husband, John, both sacral and heart chakras were being slowly restored after the loss of their infant son.

Gemma and John had hoped to expand their family. Their four-year-old daughter, Madeline, was thriving physically and emotionally, and John's commitment as a professor at a university in Paris was coming to a close. When they successfully became pregnant a second time, they decided to return to the United States where they could buy a home, place Madeline into primary school, and move through Gemma's pregnancy gracefully. John accepted a new teaching position in California and the family relocated to a beautiful, sprawling home well suited for children. Gemma's pregnancy was right on cue and mother and baby were both growing without any challenges. When John and Gemma learned that the baby was a boy, they lovingly created the new baby's nursery. They had the walls painted a light blue, bought a new bassinet, and moved the rocking chair from Madeline's room to a spot by the window in the nursery. Just when everything was ready for the baby's arrival, Gemma went into a traditional labor—her water broke and she and John calmly drove to the hospital for the baby's delivery. Gemma and baby were placed on a heart rate monitor and everything progressed beautifully.

Several hours later, in a silent recovery room, Gemma and John learned that their beloved baby boy had been born still. There was no cause. No reason. They returned home from the hospital without their baby.

When I met with Gemma, six months later, her hair had begun to gray at the top of her crown, and the corners of her eyes kept a crease that suggested she was older than her age. Her sacral chakra, still soft, was gently concealed by the layers of a scarf and cardigan sweater. It was difficult for me not to weep with her as we opened the reading in search of meaning.

Immediately, I saw her son, now in spirit, behind her. Gemma was moving through grief, but he had chosen to stay with her until she could find solace. He explained that neither she or John had done anything wrong, and in fact, another baby was already "lined up" to come to fruition for them. I was shown that although deeply sad, the baby had chosen to return home to Heaven at the very last minute, so as not to cause Gemma and John additional heartbreak. I was shown that the baby, had he stayed, would have developed severe challenges with his heart. It was fated that only weeks later, despite round-the-clock care, he would inevitably cross over. So, rather than crossing over later, the baby chose to depart at his first opportunity. He went on to share that he loves Gemma, John, and Madeline, and has already committed to returning to the family in about thirty years; next time, as a son to Madeline. When I was shown this information, I paused from my reading to define soul groups and soul contracts to Gemma . . .

The spirit or soul is infinite. Think about that for a moment. You, at your essence, are infinite. Your body inevitably dies; however, your soul is eternal. Your soul is always whole, perfect, and complete. Always. When it returns to Heaven, through angelic escort, it is polished to its most joyful state. Our most joyful and loving state is our most authentic self. It is actually *who* we are. With that in mind, you have the ability to influence with whom and when you would like to (re)incarnate on the Earth; however, each and every relationship that we encounter acts to teach us something sacred.

> All the world's a stage,
> And all the men and women
>   merely players;
> They have their exits and their
>   entrances,
> And one man in his time plays
>   many parts . . .
> —*AS YOU LIKE IT*, WILLIAM SHAKESPEARE

There are several archetypes of the soul. In my experience in my practice, the three most common are the Brave Soul, the Teacher Soul, and the Healer Soul.

Some clients have moved through trauma, abuse, addiction, war, or heinous atrocities. In general, these brave souls have come to the Earth, this time, to learn about power, oppression, fear, or anger.

Some clients have moved through challenges with their

health such as sickness, disease, or mental illness. The souls, generally speaking, have agreed to act as teachers in their closest relationships. They teach empathy, respect, and compassion.

Some clients have volunteered as souls to be healers. Typically, healers land in families that are wrought with dysfunction or limiting beliefs. Healers take on lessons of the heart until they develop boundaries and learn to protect themselves and their light.

No matter the role which we, as souls, elect to play this lifetime, we are all learning. The trick, as I have observed, is to learn with the most love and light, and the least amount of pain and suffering.

Pain and suffering, while uncomfortable, can be utilized as great opportunities to learn, however. Oftentimes, we become so complacent in our lives, or we allow others to take away our power to the extent that we overlook our own purpose. We are given opportunities again and again to make changes in our lives. I like to say, "God *whispers* His intentions for us." But it is up to us to listen. If we refuse to listen, then His messages become increasingly loud in our lives, so much so that they can come in the form of a *wallop*—redirecting us and our path in one fell swoop. Therefore, pain has a purpose.

The group of souls that we choose to learn with in this lifetime is also part of a soul contract. A glimpse into your soul contract can be analyzed by looking at your Akashic Records with a Medium, a reading of your astrological chart, or simply understanding the most influential relationships in our lives.

If your soul has agreed to play a role, then we can possibly think of the soul contract as the script for that role. Yes, you may choose to put your own spin on your costume, study the role carefully, or ad lib as you go, but for the most part, the script dictates the outcome of your part. In effect, we have both: free will and fate.

In the case of Gemma and John, they had agreed, on a soul-contract level, to take on the possibility that their baby boy would cross over in his infancy, and abruptly. In doing so, Gemma's and John's hearts were broken, while their baby returned home to Heaven without having to endure his own physical heart battles in the body. An incredible lesson that broke open the love for their children beyond space and time.

> I don't know if we each have a destiny, or if we're all just floating around accidental-like on a breeze. But I think maybe it's both. Maybe both is happening at the same time.
> —*FORREST GUMP*, BY WINSTON GROOM

It is possible to remember, on a soul level, some past-life relationships. For example, one soul will take on the physical attributes of a son. In another lifetime, that same soul may take on the attributes of being the father. One soul can take on many different roles, however each lifetime presents lessons through the lens of that specific gender, race, or religion.

Gemma and John's beautiful baby boy will return through the family's biological line: next time as a grandson.

In 2015, by the time the children were out of school for the summer, referrals from friends and family started to grow far beyond what I was comfortable with having at my home. I needed a professional space where clients could come to see me without having to step over the bicycles on the sidewalk or the soccer ball in the yard. Having to keep the front of the house neat and tidy all the time had grown old, and it was time again to step into my power.

For several months I had been casually looking for an office to rent, but the right one, at the right place, at the right budget, had not opened up yet. Then one day a friend called and said she had spoken to the owner of a beautiful Victorian-style house on Market Street that was available for rent. I negotiated with the owners and after many months of the house lying vacant, we agreed on a price and signed the lease.

I was so excited to offer a private and professional space where my clients and I could meet. Every day, I raced to prepare. I posted an ad in the local newspaper for a Grand Opening and invited everyone I knew. The office on Market Street proved to be the perfect setting for the forthcoming thousands of readings that I would offer there. I was starting to understand the power of prayer, the power of manifestation, and the power of my own spirit.

One afternoon, while working at the office, the phone rang, and I gladly answered. "Hello, this is Annemarie," I said.

"Hello, um . . . Hi, Annemarie. My name is Arjun Sharma, and I would like to schedule an appointment with you. My father has recently passed away and I hope you can get some answers for me from him."

"Oh, sure, Arjun. It will be great to work together, and I am sure I can connect you with your dad."

I quickly placed his name in my schedule and with that, another new client was booked. I looked forward to working with him, as I did every new client.

Two weeks later, Arjun came to my office for the first time. I had not given it any thought in advance, but I had not expected him to be as handsome and charismatic as he was. Immediately we clicked, and I surprised myself by how attracted I was to him. He was tall with a gleaming smile and bright brown eyes. I knew in an instant he was a healer and had already committed to working with angels in this lifetime. When we sat together at my desk to begin his reading, we held hands and prayed together to invoke the angels and his support from spirit—as I did with every client. I did not expect an energy to zing through our hands and race to my heart, making it skip a beat. Before the prayer was through, I opened my eyes and quickly shut them again to see if he had experienced the same sensations. *Focus, Annemarie,* I said to myself. I knew this reading would be special, but I did not yet know how.

Arjun's father stepped forward into the reading with ease. Arjun seemed accustomed to readings and shared that he had worked with a wonderful tarot card reader for many years in Philadelphia. "But nothing like this," he said. His heart was still in grief, and he was worried that his father's aggressive colon cancer would be something that might be hereditary. I looked into the future and confirmed that Arjun would be free and clear of any risks of developing colon cancer, should he continue to maintain a healthy lifestyle. He was an exceptionally busy man, often working late into the night as a surgeon at a local hospital. Sometimes he erred on the side of not getting adequate rest and not eating healthy foods so he could work longer. I reinforced that my readings are based on the energy of that moment in time, and if he wanted to change the trajectory even more, he could. It was his choice.

When I was looking into the health history of Arjun's father, I noted particularly clear images of his internal organs. I explained how the cancer started and how it spread. It was ironic, I thought, that Arjun's father crossed over from the exact same kind of cancer that Arjun frequently removes from his patients.

As smart and as educated as he was, Arjun was restless now that his father had crossed over. He had always turned to him for guidance. Now, Arjun would be faced with making his decisions on his own, as well as stepping into the role of caregiver for his mother. He had spent so much time and attention focused on his education, fellowship, and residency; he had little time left over to commit to serious romantic relationships. He worried if he would ever become a father. I looked again into the future and assured him that he would, in fact, begin his family a little later than most men, but would be healthy and successful. He was pleased to be able to connect with his father in spirit, look into the future for his health and family, and assured me he would be back again soon for additional readings. Arjun's father encouraged him to create the life he wanted, to be creative, and to "go after" his dreams. With time and a little more reassurance, I knew that he would step into his own power.

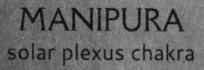

MANIPURA

solar plexus chakra

3

THE SOLAR PLEXUS CHAKRA

> **Power is given only to those who dare to lower themselves and pick it up. Only one thing matters, one thing; to be able to dare!**
>
> **—FYODOR DOSTOEVSKY**

UNFINISHED BUSINESS

The agreements that we create in past lives often perpetuate into our soul's DNA in our current lifetime. Some call it karma. Karma is said to be an action or deed that results in consequences. Oftentimes in popular culture, the word "karma" has a negative connotation. While not exactly correct, there is some amount of truth to our actions and deeds and the energetic consequences tied to them.

The third chakra, or the solar plexus, is located in the center of our bodies. Like the sun, it is where our physical, emotional, and spiritual power is stored. It is also where the etheric cords of attachment are located in the energetic field.

When I began working with Julia, a well-respected and successful businesswoman, I clairvoyantly saw her working through a web of entanglements. It was as though a spider had spun an elaborate cobweb around her—so much so that everything she did, every decision that she made, was filtered through the sticky webs. Over time, this acted like a screen that obstructed her view, and she was no longer able to see clearly. By any given day's end, she was exhausted and drained. Soon, she began to rely on prescription medication to give her energy to "get through the day."

Julia and I began working closely to unravel the web, and piece by piece, I was shown how her third chakra—her personal autonomy and power—was embedded behind generations of power struggles.

Julia's father, Frederick, also a well-known and respected businessman, had battled and overcome addictions to pain medications and alcohol. Battles, hard fought, that Julia witnessed as a young girl. She saw the contradiction in her father's life—outward success, internal strife. When her father was admitted to rehabilitation, he was able to release his chemical dependencies. Upon returning to his home and work as a Mercedes-Benz salesman, however, he was continuously challenged professionally until he opened his own car dealership with an up-and-coming colleague, Clark.

At first, Fred and Clark's car dealership flourished. Clark was a young and ambitious businessman and Fred had hoped he would bring enthusiasm into his already well-established base of customers. Not long after they entered into their contract, Clark began to claim Fred's customers as his own, and soon a power struggle ensued. Again, Fred found himself feeling powerless, and he was pushed toward an early retirement, allowing Clark to take over the dealership entirely.

By the time Julia had completed college and earned a master's of business administration from a prestigious university, Clark's dealership was bursting at the seams. Julia now had an executive-level education and Clark needed a savvy business partner to offset the number of customers he was serving. As fate would have it, Julia was available. Julia signed an agreement with Clark, despite her father's warning, and she moved forward as a "partner" in the dealership.

Clark's power plays that once pushed Fred around looked a lot like being a boss to Julia, at first. He had a bigger office, a bigger bonus, more vacation time, and a much bigger cut of that "partnership." Even though Clark had agreed to making her a partner, Julia often felt overlooked and disrespected.

"How did I get into this mess, Annemarie?" she asked, taking off her glasses and wringing her hands.

The dichotomy of her father's model was now showing up for Julia. The outward appearance of success was increasingly in conflict with Julia's internal knowledge. It was as though she had been baited—and now, her promised dealership had been switched. She felt obligated to Clark for "giving her a start" and guilty and embarrassed for not "heeding Dad's caution." She had already signed a lengthy contract that included a "do not compete" clause within a twenty-five-mile radius of the dealership. I turned to her guardian angels for support.

I saw that the power struggles between Julia and Clark were residual karmic relationships—unfinished business, so to speak, from her father. In fact, if Fred had referred to his contract with Clark and hired an attorney to speak on his behalf, Fred would have been able to retire *and* maintain a stake in the business, therefore leveraging his personal power and applying it in the instance with Clark. Instead, the intergenerational lesson had been passed down to Julia.

"You mean, I have to stand up to him? I have to stand up to Clark?" she asked.

"Yes," I said directly. "Your father had one opportunity, and because he did not take it, now that opportunity is passed on to you. In order to correct the lesson of power in your family's energetic line, you can choose to assert yourself and reclaim what is rightfully yours. It is your free-will choice, however."

"But if I do not choose to reclaim my authority over this mess, what will happen?"

"Then the lesson of reclaiming your power will be presented to you again. The lesson does not go away. In fact, it just manifests in different ways."

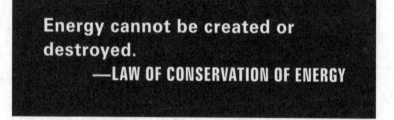

Energy cannot be created or destroyed.
—LAW OF CONSERVATION OF ENERGY

My reading with Julia prompted a review of my own challenges with personal power passed down from my parents. Over the years, I had witnessed how my mother and father gave and took within their marriage. Mom modeled the behavior of consistently erring on the side of forgiveness and passivity. So, when Dad dropped the ball, Mom was often left picking up the pieces.

Christopher, Maria, and Anna were changing and growing quickly, and I was working hard to honor my commitment to myself to have honesty and authenticity at home. When the divorce documents drifted back and forth for almost two years, I realized it was time that I put an end to the purgatory and stand up for myself and the kids once and for all. I needed to move forward, and the lingering cords of attachment were preventing me from doing so.

My attorney, Lisa, and I met together on a cold and dark evening just before my birthday in November of 2015. The week after daylight savings begins and the clocks fall back an hour, makes for unexpected darkness by 5:00 P.M. The leaves, now fallen, whirled across the city sidewalks as I hurried to meet Lisa at her office downtown. The long oval conference table sat dimly lit before a wall of windows overlooking the state capitol building in Harrisburg, Pennsylvania. I waited patiently for her arrival.

"It's good to see you, Annemarie!" Lisa said with a smile as she sat down across from me. "You look good . . . better," she said, nodding her head in approval.

"I am starting to eat again," I said quietly, to validate her observation. During the worst times, I could not stomach much food, and my weight dwindled considerably. I recall there were many days that I ate nothing at all due to pangs of grief in my stomach. I felt like all authority over my life and children had been terminated and I was at the whim of the wind. Although I had promised and committed to pursue the work of Mediumship, I had yet to feel squarely safe. I knew, though, that whatever was before me, it had to be better than what was behind me.

"If you could, please sign here and here," Lisa said, angling her glasses to the edge of her nose as she reviewed the last of the divorce and custody agreements. "These documents confirm that you are agreeing to primary physical custody of Christopher, Maria, and Anna, and that Doyle will assume custody every other Friday beginning at five thirty P.M. into Saturday. It will be your responsibility to pick the children up on Sunday evenings at seven P.M. I know Doyle had originally requested nine P.M, but your request for seven was permitted so the kids can get settled in for school on Monday morning. Holidays and vacation are also broken down into Holiday A and Holiday B schedules. You will have two nonconsecutive weeks of vacation with the kids each year."

I was listening carefully, but I began to drift out of my body. I looked out at the shadows now cast upon the steps to the capitol. Snow flurries began to fall and whip around the lampposts.

Lisa handed me a pen. "Annemarie . . . please . . . your signature and then we are all done."

While the children were under my roof, I knew there

would be fourteen more Christmases for Anna, twelve more Easters for Maria, and eight more Thanksgivings for Christopher, but the familiar hollowness in my stomach returned as I knew I would not be able to share in the joy for all of them. I signed the final draft of the divorce documents. And I felt as though my dream of having a big family had died.

I was beside myself again for several more weeks. The winding path out of grief spiraled back to the beginning, and I spent the Christmas morning of 2015 in bed weeping while the kids began their new back-and-forth holiday schedule.

I wished I could have been more like Mom, turning a blind eye to any indiscretion. Or maybe I should have been more like Dad and never tolerated anything at all, ever. Mom suggested that I do "anything to keep the family together" while Dad said that I should have "ended it long ago."

Holidays came and went, and Doyle frequently seemed to be unavailable to spend time with the kids. It felt to me like adding insult to injury, and I decided that I wanted to develop new traditions—not just for me, but for the kids.

One rainy day, the kids were watching the movie *Mrs. Doubtfire,* and my ears perked up from across the room while I was washing dishes. It was Robin Williams again—this time his character said, "There are all sorts of different families . . . Some families have one mommy, some families have one daddy, or two families. And some children live with their uncle or aunt. Some live with their grandparents, and some children live with foster parents. And some live in separate homes, in separate neighborhoods, in different areas of the country—and they may not see each other for days, or weeks, months . . . even years at a time. But if there's love, dear . . . those are the ties that bind, and you'll have a family in your heart, forever."

Mrs. Doubtfire's advice struck a chord with me. I knew I had to begin to define this new reality for myself. *How can I begin to restore my power in my family? In myself?* I wondered.

I referred back to my chakra books, and it dawned on me. I realized that I had exhausted myself by attempting to help and even to heal Doyle. The therapy, the love, the patience, the kindness. But nothing seemed to make everything better. I knew it was not up to me to be responsible for Doyle's actions. That was his job. But I knew I had to be extremely accountable for my own actions. In order to balance my third chakra, and those of my children, I needed more light in.

I talked to Julia about power and the ways in which we can compromise our own power. Sometimes we diminish our own power with our contracts: physical or spiritual. Other times we give away our power by not practicing discernment over healthy boundaries. Julia began working in tandem with a clinical psychologist. Together, they developed a plan that empowered Julia to approach Clark, appeal the existing agreement, and design a new contract that would be consistent with what Julia wanted.

The third chakra encourages us to develop individuation—a process by which Julia successfully identified her blind spots and was able to overcome patterns from her family.

ANAHATA
heart chakra

4

THE HEART CHAKRA

LOVE OR FEAR

Family patterns extend beyond matters of power and often overlap with matters of the heart. As I continued to learn about my own personal power, I also learned about what stirred my heart. While my romantic relationship with Doyle had ended many years ago, my heart was recovering from the breakup of my family. I was moving forward, steadier and stronger, and took great comfort in the love I have for Christopher, Maria, and Anna. Slowly, I began to see that, like petals on a rose, love unfolds in our lives in many different ways. For me, the love I have for my children took center stage. And the clusters of clients that came forth aligned with that same energy.

The first time I saw Sophia Affeto, I loved her the way I loved my third-grade teacher. She was warm and welcoming with a big smile, rosy cheeks, and large-framed glasses that accentuated her brown eyes. She entered my office on an October Saturday morning when all the red and golden leaves whirled around the front porch of my office. As I opened the door to greet her, I did not see or feel a wisp of a reason as to why she would be coming to see me. She was one "bouquet of pencils" away from being Meg Ryan's character in *You've Got Mail* or a beloved fairy-tale princess in a Disney classic.

As we sat down together at my oval office table and began our reading together with my prayer, I could see that Sophia closed her eyes and held tightly to my hands. Her guardian angels and deceased family members began to fill the space in front of me and behind me. I immediately recognized that her father-in-law would be with us for the duration of the reading. I knew that she was deeply protected and respected by her angels and that she was already serving her life purpose work as a teacher and mother.

Her father-in-law was dutiful, kind, and articulate. I could see how his presence linked Sophia to her spouse, Alberto, and their three children. They were truly a beautiful family, and their life was an uncommon success story. While Sophia worked as a science teacher at a local middle school, Alberto worked tirelessly and diligently to provide a beautiful and comfortable home and lifestyle. They were a dream team together, who laughed through the adventures of parenthood. In the wake of my divorce, my snapshot into their life together knocked on the door to my own heart that had been quietly closed to romantic love by grief. My children would never come to know the safety of a two-parent household like Sophia and Alberto's. I squeezed Sophia's hands to return my focus toward her path and her angel's messages.

"We'll start with the heart," her angels told me. And we did.

In advance of our reading, Sophia called to inquire about how things work for me. Would the reading compromise her faith in Christ and contradict the teachings of her church? I assured her, "Not only is it in alignment with the teachings of Christianity, I've found that it will also affirm your beliefs in God, the Universe, and love."

Her profound faith had guided her life, her marriage, and her motherhood. Until recently, her faith had offered steadfast responses to her calls for support or direction. Now, however, it seemed that her faith was being tested by an unexpected lesson.

Alberto Jr., or "A.J." as they called him, the only son and oldest of her three children, had recently moved to Colorado to establish himself with his new wife. He loved hiking and biking and was the all-American kind of guy that would make any mom's heart sing. He was tall and handsome, well educated, and on his way to repeat the success that his parents' actions modeled for him. When he married and moved to Colorado, Sophia and Alberto never suspected that their new daughter-in-law, Morgan, would slowly and quietly tug A.J. toward an astringent lifestyle of extremes. What appeared to be a harmless introduction to an organic lifestyle quickly led A.J. down the rabbit hole of a monitored and rigid routine that ultimately led to Morgan's complete control of not only A.J. but their new baby, as well. Sophia offered her love at first, of course, followed by a fleeting phase of disbelief. "How can this be happening?" she asked. An intuitive mother, Sophia fore-saw that Morgan would continue to police A.J.'s conversations with his mom back east and push Sophia out of her son's and granddaughter's lives.

Our intuition was right.

Within months I clairvoyantly saw that Morgan's demands would further isolate A.J. and completely cut off communication with Sophia, Alberto, and their two daughters on the East Coast. For Sophia, this imminent consequence left her feeling helpless and heartbroken.

Three years passed by.

Holidays, birthdays, anniversaries. No contact. It was as if Sophia had been hit by a car, and moved through her day in a state of confusion. Without any clear answers to her questions and without any real footing to move forward, she stayed in a period of internal conflict. What had she done that could have possibly caused this? On the outside, one would still perceive her as the beautiful, capable, loving teacher and mother. But internally, a war within her heart had begun.

Every few months, Sophia came for a reading to check in on her son. I saw that he was safe, thriving in his career, and had taken to being a father in the same manner that Alberto had modeled for him. Her guardian angels insisted that she not give up hope, and guided her, through our readings, to write to him by email or letters. She did, and she prayed every day that A.J. would return home.

A.J.'s two sisters' lives continued. There were weddings and the arrival of new babies. Sophia loved seeing her daughters grow into maturity, but her heart still ached for A.J. As she neared her retirement from teaching, it was another milestone moment that proved too much for her, and high blood pressure and routine heart palpitations sent her to see the cardiologist. There, the doctor identified that Sophia had a completely blocked artery and needed heart surgery and a stent. Quickly, the family scrambled to get Sophia the care she needed, despite it being a relatively low-risk, routine procedure.

While Sophia was in the operating room, her heart stopped, and she crossed over on the operating room table.

Seconds passed and Sophia's heart began again. Her team of physicians succeeded in moving forward with her procedure, and she was monitored carefully in the intensive care unit.

Alberto and the family had been waiting at the hospital during Sophia's operation. Upon learning how the surgery transpired, Alberto phoned A.J. and left a voicemail for him.

Less than twelve hours later, while Sophia was still in recovery, A.J. returned home to see his mother. He apologized profusely for having placed his mother and father in such duress for so long. He had received every single email and letter that Sophia had sent him.

A.J. went into further detail, that he had wanted to separate from Morgan but was too terrified to do so with their daughter being in jeopardy of experiencing Morgan's narcissistic abuse. With Alberto and Sophia's support, the family came together and effortlessly began to heal. Soon, A.J. and his daughter moved back to the East Coast where Sophia and Alberto, now retired, see them routinely.

The heart chakra involves learning the ways in which we can move forward without causing any harm. The heart chakra is located in the center of our physical bodies and in the center of our spiritual body. Our arms, once extended left and right, expand the energy of the heart chakra as far, if not farther, than we can reach. The etheric pathways in and around our bodies flow freely, enabling a sense of balance between the chakras of the body below and the chakras of the spirit above.

In Sanskrit, the word "anahata" translates to the heart chakra. It means "the sound that is made without any two things striking."

Ultimately, for Sophia Affeto, it was her heart that brought her family together again. There is no doubt that her steadfast love and commitment to family, is a teacher to us all.

> **i carry your heart with me (i carry it in my heart)**
>
> —E. E. CUMMINGS

Many of the classes that I offer begin with a guided meditation. Like poetry, a guided meditation can transport us into a different time and space. I often speak of flowers in my meditations, in part because they are beautiful, but also because of their impermanence. I always associate the heart chakra with roses, as they should be, in my opinion, the center of every garden. Roses in particular offer brilliant buds and an enchanting fragrance. But they, too, have too short of a season.

Libi Goldman used to arrive at my office a little early just so she could sit on the front porch on the wicker bench and admire the rosebushes. Her black hair gently framed her face and a few strands of early gray presented at her crown. I would peek through the window to see her peacefully and patiently waiting for her turn. Libi is an exceptionally thoughtful person and often surprised me with gifts. One year, we happened to schedule a reading on my birthday, and she arrived with a beautiful piece of cake with two sliced strawberries gently placed in the center to form a red heart. In another instance, she gave me a bleeding-heart houseplant for my windowsill that had long, arching stems that reached the floor. These kind gestures were always appreciated, and I hoped that our sessions gave her the gift of peace. For nearly two decades, she had carried an overwhelming sense of grief as a result of her only sister's abrupt loss.

Libi had shared a bedroom with her sister, Eden, all while growing up. They were both successful students and active in sports, including field hockey teams. They fought over favorite clothes, makeup, and hair accessories—as normal teenagers do. Their parents kept healthy, busy lives between work and taking care of their immaculate ranch-style home. Eden was really funny, often cracking jokes and pulling harmless pranks. Together, they were the girls next door. There was no way of knowing that Libi would come home from school one day to find her adoring sister, Eden, had taken her life. Libi found her lifeless in their bedroom. It was utterly devastating to Libi, their family, and the community.

Before long, Libi was so affected by Eden's death that she

suffered severe heart complications, including cardiomyopathy resulting in a heart attack—or in layman's terms, a broken heart. Since Eden's death, Libi carried the enormity of the trauma and grief with her everywhere. When I clairvoyantly investigated Libi's story, I was humbled to see the expansive depth and breadth of love Libi held for Eden. As Eden's spirit entered our readings, I was surprised at how similar they looked—their likeness was unmistakable. Eden offered shared memories that only Libi knew of, which quickly validated her presence. She also often sang songs or recited lyrics that had special meaning to Libi. And although it was not necessary for me to understand the significance, all that mattered was that I was getting Eden's messages across clearly.

Eden insisted that there was never anything that Libi could have or should have done differently. In fact, Eden revealed that her suicide had actually been a half-hearted attempt— and she had never intended to follow through. She also revealed that she wanted Libi to know that she was, in fact, in Heaven. Furthermore, Eden impressed upon me to assure her sister that both she and Libi would be reunited again in Heaven—when the time was right.

She went on to show me how big the energy of the heart really is. And how important it is to understand that under no circumstances would Libi's love and connection to Eden ever be severed. Eden emphatically encouraged Libi to continue to process her grief in a gentle manner, but to not *stay* in grief—as she had willingly for so long now. Libi had been unable to move forward with her own personal goals—education, career, relationships—as a result of holding on to the grief. By holding on to the grief, Libi felt as though she would hold on to Eden.

Consequently, her physical heart gave way. The depth of grief, while never really gone, is only ever intended to be a temporary emotion. The expansive heart chakra is so big, that grief and joy can coexist.

Libi and I continued to work together for several more sessions, carefully taking clairvoyant looks into what possibilities she had in the future. For the first time in many years, she explored a new job—one that was a bit out of her comfort zone—where she met a new love interest, and they began to date. Libi reported seeing and feeling signs from Eden quite often and was so happy to have validation from our sessions that they were in fact not coincidences, but the spirit of her sister saying hello.

I will never forget sharing the message to Libi from Eden that "Grief and joy can coexist."

How is it possible that the heart chakra can be so seemingly simple yet completely complex? I wondered.

In my line of work, it is not entirely unusual for "work" to come home with me. From time to time, a deceased family member of a client will stop by my home in advance of a reading, so as to get to know me a little. They do their homework, so to speak. That way, when it is time for me to connect with their family members here on Earth, the connection is clear. I liken it to high-speed internet versus dial-up. It helps everyone involved to have a secure line.

Libi's sister Eden, in addition to my guardian angels and family members in Heaven, was one to frequent my home and offer drops of divine advice regarding my own healing heart. She suggested I take some time for myself and listen to my heart.

After Doyle and I had rounded the corner of our divorce agreement and finalized the children's custody stipulation, I realized I had been working so hard that I had not made time to process my feelings. Eden had been right. I had already moved through denial and bargaining in the years before the split, and now that the shock of the separation had passed, depression was setting in. My network of support was changing too, especially since Candy had crossed over. I felt like an astronaut in outer space barely tethered to the space shuttle and drifting farther from home. I dated but kept meeting the same kind of men: they were possessive, told half-truths, raced to marry me, or kept me at their beck and call. I was seeking balance, but the Universe was showing me extremes. Once I caught on to the patterns, I realized I still had a lot to learn about protecting my sacred heart and boundaries, speaking up, and speaking my truth. I needed a time-out from romantic relationships, so I turned to another love: my books, instead.

Back when I was a junior at Rollins College in Winter Park, Florida, I took an early-Saturday-morning Shakespeare class. Mornings in central Florida in the early spring are the jewels of nature. Especially at Rollins. Bent old oak trees that wore Spanish moss felt more like my friends that had come home from a night out on the town—still dressed up in their heels and wearing their bling as they tiptoed back to their dorm. The brick campus roads were neatly fitted along Lake Virginia where, just before the bell rang, Dr. Victoria Romano would slide her classic red convertible Jaguar into a parking spot and sail into her classroom.

"Good morning, Dr. Romano," I would say as I walked quickly ahead of her so as not to be the last student to enter the classroom.

"Good morning," she would reply with her sunglasses still on, reaching for her oversized bag of books, while slipping off her scarf. She was half professor, half Audrey Hepburn.

Her classroom was always full, and students squeezed into the wooden chairs encircling the grand oak table where all of us gathered around.

Dr. Romano might as well have been Juliet Capulet herself, but her star-crossed love affair was not with Romeo. Dr. Romano's love was her books.

As classmates were called upon to read portions of Shakespeare, Dr. Romano often stood at the head of the table and silently recited the words, line by line, from memory. One day, she opened a window for us to see into her past and shared that at one time, she had committed to being a nun and vowed a path of service. Not long after she made her promise, she met her husband, left the church, and married. Years later, as she was seeking her PhD and met with the demands of a family, Victoria found herself sneaking off to read her beloved Shakespeare. Her husband accused her of cheating, but in fact, her desire had simply shifted to the love of her work. Headstrong and determined, at the height of her obligations, she left her husband, and earned her doctorate.

Dr. Romano's story came to mind again at just the right time for me and influenced my decision to take a step away from dating, for a while, at least, and focus entirely on my research, work, and of course my children, where my heart could safely be at peace.

> **There is no greater agony than bearing an untold story inside you.**
>
> **—MAYA ANGELOU**

I was on my way to a meeting, racing down the winding roads of my country town, when out of nowhere, a police officer spun out of a hidden gravel drive to catch me speeding.

"Where are you heading in such a hurry, miss?" he asked.

"I am so sorry, Officer. I have a meeting to get to and work to do," I responded with a lump in my throat as tears began to well up in my eyes.

"There's nothing so important that you can't slow down. It's for your own safety," he said. And with that, he issued a ticket and a steep fine. I sat along the side of the road and cried, called to reschedule my meeting, and returned home to cry some more.

While I was seated on my family room sofa, a gentle warmth came over me. My tears subsided and I clairaudiently heard, "You have got to slow down. You are not taking this seriously enough." And I nodded in humility and apologized quietly as I wiped the tears from my cheeks. I had thought that I was doing what I had been guided to do. But, slowing down or going slowly had never been my pace. I had so much to learn, but racing from one commitment to the next was not exactly what the fine print of my agreement to "do this work" had stated. I had been offering readings to so many clients, but still not applying what I had been witnessing for myself.

Well, shit, I thought. *You can't pour from an empty cup, damn it.* And I took the remainder of the day to rest and think carefully about stillness, slowing down, and how I could keep my cup full, so to speak.

The following morning, as I prepared for my 10:00 A.M. client to arrive, I felt a foreboding heaviness in my chest. I knew it was an indication that my client had a lot to say—a lot to "get off her chest."

Antonina stood tall and slender in my office with knee-high black leather boots and a stylish black leather jacket. Her hair was as black as a raven's feather with hints of magenta and purple. She wore thick eyeliner that reminded me of the Egyptian queen Cleopatra and spoke loudly, in a heavy Ukrainian accent. Her energy immediately dominated the office, and I felt like a wilted flower sitting across from her. I knew already that she carried this oppressive cloak of energy with her everywhere as a means of protection. *But why?* I wondered.

As we officially began the reading, a man in spirit entered the office and stood right behind me. It was her late husband, also a man from the Ukraine, with whom Antonina shared a daughter.

As I introduced him, Antonina insisted that she "had nothing to say to him, whatsoever!" and asked that I move forward with the reading, excluding him from the messages. I paused for a moment and said, "He's here today to ask you for forgiveness." And with that, Antonina's anger began to quake within her throat.

"Annamarie," she said, "he abandoned us. He left me and my daughter with nothing. Nothing. I refuse. I refuse to forgive him." As she spoke, her jaw tightened, and her eyes narrowed.

Ivan, her husband, went on to explain to me that Antonina was correct. He had not been there for her, or their newborn baby. He left them penniless to run rampant with alcohol and drugs, cheating on her many times, until Antonina found the courage to leave their home and move to the United States, taking her daughter with her. Ivan had made several attempts at contacting her by phone, but as confused and desperate as she was, Antonina was determined to escape the broken promises and manipulation. Soon after she and her daughter had established a small studio apartment, she learned that Ivan had taken his life.

For over twenty-six years, Antonina had carried the grief silently. She had never spoken of Ivan to anyone, not even her daughter. Ever. And she had never offered forgiveness to him.

As I sat at my office table that morning, watching the miraculous opportunity for peace unfold before my eyes, I knew why my guardian angels had guided me to sit still and rest the day before. They were preparing me for the weight of twenty-six years of anger, sadness, grief, confusion, and shame to be confronted that day with Antonina.

It was amazing, actually. I clairvoyantly saw impressions of trauma and hardships that Antonina faced and endured as a new mother, working and raising a child all by herself in a country where she did not speak the language, but sought as a refuge for peace and safety.

Antonina had made an incredibly brave choice. Ivan showed me how proud he was of their daughter, who had recently become a resident physician at a hospital in Philadelphia.

"Yes," Antonina replied, looking me in the eye. "I am so proud of her, Annamarie. We have worked so hard. So, so hard," she said. "We never stopped working."

In the corner of my mind, Antonina's voice echoed, *We never stopped working,* and I redirected my attention to the future trajectory for her. Just yesterday, my own angels had impressed upon me the need for rest and restoration. I was beginning to be shown why for myself, as well.

Now in her early fifties, Antonina still looked young and vivacious. But her life force energy, stifled by years and years of silence and unforgiveness, was starting to take a toll on her.

As with all predictions, when I see momentum in my readings, it is based on several factors. The past does not have to influence our future, but it is our responsibility to choose a path that is one of love and peace. For Antonina, I saw that it was imperative that she shift her attention to her own health and well-being. I saw that soon, she would not be able to work, and that her guardian angels would give her a series of "speeding tickets" to get her to slow down. After twenty-six years of shielding her pain and silencing her sadness, I was shown that it would be a slow process for her to begin to release the past. *Naturally,* I thought.

Beautifully and eloquently, her guardian angels showed me

that it was time to thank her toughness and perseverance—her shield that kept her and her daughter safe—and now she had permission to rest.

"You have permission to rest," I told her.

Antonina stood up from our reading and said that she had "a lot to think about," and thanked me for being clear and direct with her.

Several months later, she called and made a follow-up appointment. This time, she arrived at my office with her left arm in a sling, badly broken. She looked worried and anxious for her arm to heal so she could return to work as a hairdresser in her busy salon.

Once we were fully immersed into the reading, I saw that her broken arm was exactly the "speeding ticket" that her guardian angels had hinted at in our initial reading. Although uncomfortable, it gave her just the time-out and the time away from work that her spirit was calling for. Her guardian angels urged her to continue to rest and recover and to offer herself compassion. The busy salon had acted as a buffer for years so that Antonina would be distracted from her emotions—which had been resting dormant in her throat chakra.

I saw, clairvoyantly, that the broken arm was not ever meant to be a punishment—she had done nothing wrong. The arms are an extension of the heart chakra and act as a bridge of expression between our heart and our throat. It was, however, an opportunity for stillness. An invitation. It was up to Antonina to sit still and listen.

Several more months passed, and a third call to meet with Antonina came in. This time, her arm had healed, but thyroid cancer had developed in her throat. She understood now why her guardian angels had guided her to rest and recover. She moved into the thyroid cancer, leaning on her angels more than ever before. She was grateful I had introduced them to her in our readings. She developed a time for daily meditation and prayer. In our third reading together, I saw that yes, in fact, the operation to remove the malignant tumors would be successful, and that she would move through treatments bravely, and victorious.

When I met with Antonina a fourth and final time, I saw that all of her fear, worry, grief, and inability to forgive Ivan had collected at the base of her throat—precisely where the tumors were successfully removed. Headstrong at first, once she had permission, she sat silently, without distractions, and moved through the layers of forgiveness necessary to move forward. After her surgery and oncology treatments were complete, she recovered, moved to Philadelphia to be closer to her daughter, and started a whole new life, again, this time with acceptance, forgiveness, and joy.

I could not help but think about the "speeding tickets" my guardian angels had given me. Opportunities to slow down, reflect, correct my course a bit before moving forward. As important as it was for Antonina to pause and listen, it was just as important for me to follow suit. My perception about peace and stillness began to shift. I no longer saw it as punishment for having done something wrong. Now, I saw peace and stillness as an opportunity to expand my awareness. Something that I had started to see that my guardian angels were still guiding me toward.

When Arjun called my office again, I expected him to want to schedule another reading. Instead, he called to ask me out to dinner. I was completely taken by surprise, and we made arrangements to meet at a Mediterranean restaurant right down the street from my office.

The day of our date, I felt nervous and almost talked myself out of going. We sat outside that September evening and admired the sunset together as he poured me a glass of wine. He had brought me a small box of chocolates from a recent trip to Paris to visit his brother. He was impressively confident and charming. "Annemarie, I think your work is really interesting. Tell me, do you believe in reincarnation?"

I laughed, remembering the first time I met him and the zing of energy that raced to my heart when we held hands.

"Yes, of course," I replied. And before I knew it, we had finished our Mediterranean-style entrees and sat back to open the box of chocolates. Arjun and I continued to see each other, and although he still made me nervous, we grew closer in time. Soon, he was calling every day, and we spent hours talking and getting to know each other more. Over the next year we became wonderful friends, and my once-broken heart began to soften to the possibility of love again.

VISHUDDHA
throat chakra

5

THE THROAT CHAKRA

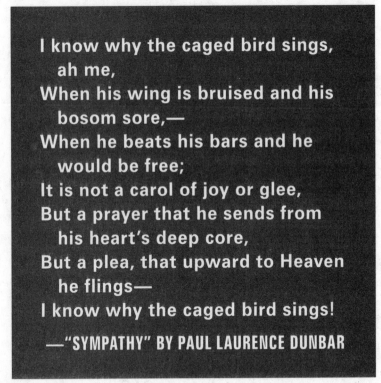

I know why the caged bird sings,
   ah me,
When his wing is bruised and his
   bosom sore,—
When he beats his bars and he
   would be free;
It is not a carol of joy or glee,
But a prayer that he sends from
   his heart's deep core,
But a plea, that upward to Heaven
   he flings—
I know why the caged bird sings!

—"SYMPATHY" BY PAUL LAURENCE DUNBAR

In November of 2011, when I experienced my Kundalini Awakening, I vividly recall the sensations of words and feelings being tightly compacted at my throat. Once the etheric energy moved through the entangled cords, I distinctly remember a feeling of freedom—as though my heart and my thoughts were flowing freely through the pipeline of the throat.

The throat chakra is an incredibly sensitive chakra. At times, it acts as a filter; if fiery feelings are best left unsaid, or when watery words flow without warning. This chakra acts as a means of protection to our more subtle senses in the sixth and seventh chakras. It allows for inward expression through our thoughts and outward expression through our voice.

Author Don Miguel Ruiz writes in his book *The Four Agreements* that we are to be "impeccable" with our words. Your word, as he says, is not only the promises we make to others, but the promises we make to ourselves.

There was a time, when I was a teenager, that I promised myself I would become a writer. I had utilized music since I was a child to buffer out the angels and spirits that beckoned my attention noon and night. Music had become a friend to me—bringing me protection and comfort, excitement or introspection. It was a natural collaboration to add writing to my music.

I would stow away in my bedroom listening to singer-songwriters like Bob Dylan and Joni Mitchell. Often, I would imagine that I would be a writer for a music magazine like *Rolling Stone* one day. There, I would work with photographer Annie Leibovitz, smoking cigarettes, wearing all black, and writing about the next big act. "The two Annies" would have backstage passes and front-row seats to all the concerts. It would be *awesome*.

When I got out of the Navy, in January of 2000, I began working at a magazine publishing company in Harrisburg and kept my eyes open for a position at their headquarters in New York City. I really wanted to live and work in the city, and I had just enough determination to make it happen. Working with photographers and designers in communications while in the Navy for four years gave me enough experience for a full-time job in the graphic design department while I began chipping away at my bachelor's degree at the local community college. It was a start, I thought, that got me one step closer to my goal of being a writer for *Rolling Stone*.

The beginnings of my professional dreams were just starting to take shape. But I had not yet learned about speaking my truth and applying healthy boundaries to protect it.

When I met Doyle, in August of 2002, I was taking small steps toward achieving my goal. I had not expressed the promise to myself to anyone, really, for fear that I would be ridiculed. But Doyle was a musician himself and played guitar in blues and rock bands, so he seemed to fit the picture. Soon, my evenings and weekends were spent attending his shows. But I still needed to complete college, and central Pennsylvania was cold, dark, and gray. When Doyle lost his job, he was presented with an opportunity to move to a new town to pursue a certification in audio engineering, so I applied to colleges close to his two choices: Nashville or Orlando. Neither Nashville or Orlando was anything like New York City, but I saw it as a chance to earn my degree and *then* start a position in the city. It felt like a bit of a detour or a roundabout way of getting to my goal, but I agreed to follow him anyway.

In the suburbs of Orlando, Rollins College accepted my credits from the community college back home and I embarked on my degree in English. I was far away from where I really wanted to be but continued to silence the voice within me. I had already spent years ignoring my intuition and gifts, so stifling my voice a little longer would not matter much, I thought.

It was not until my senior year of college that one of my professors identified that I have dyslexia, too. Just like Dad. She had been observing me all semester long and when she approached me about it, she kindly commented on how brave I was to move forward all these years while overcoming this hurdle day in and day out. I went on to have a clinical diagnosis that proved my professor's suspicions to be accurate. It all made sense, of course, and I quickly reported to Mom that I was not so dull-witted after all.

Once I began to learn about the throat chakra, it was especially valuable to me to learn strategies to keep it clear and healthy. I knew that by maintaining my throat chakra, I would be able to tune in accurately, and hear communication and guidance from my angels and spiritual support team. I learned that the throat chakra also corresponds to the second or sacral chakra. Doing just about anything creative keeps these chakras open and flowing. Expression in any form—especially writing, painting, and singing—will allow for the fullest expression of the throat chakra and for what is true and authentic to you.

The Washington Chorus, in Washington D.C., performs concerts with the National Symphony Orchestra. Vocalists there are exceptionally talented and have often prepared their entire lives for their roles. When I first met with Caroline, in

2016, I saw that she was a gifted and talented soprano singer. She had a choir of angels that rested behind her and often gave her a boost of confidence to be on stage. I was surprised to see that recently, though, Caroline had stepped away from performing. Her boyfriend of seven years had recently broken up with her and Caroline was devastated. She had hoped they would marry and start a family together. Now, at thirty-six years old, she was concerned that it would be too late for those dreams to manifest. For the first time in a long time, she was supporting herself independently, so she began working at a bank to provide additional money. Rather than participating in the chorus after work and on weekends, she went home and sought comfort through food. Quickly she had gained forty pounds—furthering her feelings of rejection and depression. She realized she needed to change some patterns but was frozen with sadness.

"Caroline!" I said. "You are like a bird! You have an incredibly beautiful voice! You are a natural on the stage and wow . . . you are so blessed as a singer!" I clairvoyantly saw Caroline performing in front of large audiences and truly embracing her authentic self with joy and ease.

"Yes," she said, smiling a bright smile shyly as her curly hair covered her cheeks.

"But I see that you have recently stepped away from the spotlight. Ah, Caroline . . . your soul is seeking rest . . . and your voice is resting, too."

"Annemarie, I have been so sad and feel as though my life is not where I thought it would be. I am thirty-six now. I thought I would be married and have children by now. My mother started our family when she was twenty-two. All my sisters are married with kids of their own."

I saw that all of Caroline's desires were just on the other side of a few, easy choices. It was the transitional time that left her feeling stalled. It was up to her, however, to make the choices, stick to them, and decide for herself what she wanted her life to look like. My role that day was simple, and I introduced her choices to her.

"You have several paths that are available to you. Let's start with your heart's desires first: love, husband, home, children. These are all attainable," I said. "If you choose to stay at your current job, working at the bank, you have a new love that will be coming to meet with you. He is an experienced executive that is also seeking a new love and a commitment, as well. The job you chose at the bank was a great choice, Caroline. It will continue to ground you, help you to feel financially supported and capable of moving forward. While your day job is important, you will continue to feel stifled without movement. Your body needs a little more time to rest and recover from your recent move, new job, and departure from your ex-boyfriend. It's like a system reset. Once you begin moving your body again, through gentle movement—walking or aerobics classes—your life force energy will slowly reawaken." I continued to share more details.

"Even then, however, I see that you will still seek fulfillment—and that comes through your voice. Singing is not an option for you, Caroline. Singing is a must! It is your soul purpose, and it brings joy to everyone that you meet.

Your voice inspires and teaches others how to use theirs. It is imperative that you return to singing one way or another."

Caroline took a big, deep breath and asked, "And what about my ex-boyfriend? Is he ever coming back?"

I clairvoyantly peered down the chronological timeline for Caroline. I saw that there would be opportunities to check in with each other, but the new love that was coming in for her at the bank would be far more aligned with her maturity and purpose.

"The relationship you have shared with your ex-boyfriend has fulfilled its purpose, Caroline. I see that you have outgrown him. There will come a time, this coming summer, that you will look back with gratitude but also assurance that it was time to part ways. Not all relationships are meant to last forever."

"What matters most, beyond all romantic relationships, is your relationship with yourself. Though you had compromised your hopes and dreams, patiently waiting for your ex-boyfriend to step up, he was not going to ever step-up. I understand that the Universe has interceded in this instance to awaken you, to call attention to your gifts as a singer, so that you will protect those gifts, making them a priority in your life."

Caroline was surprised. She had grown up in choirs her entire life, and although she never planned to stop singing, she also was not aware just how important it was that she continue.

"You have to create boundaries around your soul purpose," I told her.

"Boundaries? What does that mean?" she asked.

Boundaries, for those that are not used to utilizing them, might feel like you are being rude, or demanding. But setting boundaries is an effective way of being honest. Honest about your desires and your needs.

"The clearer the boundary, the more effectively you can honor your gift as a singer," I told her.

I went back in time to see how Caroline's parents had influenced her throat chakra. Caroline grew up in an active and healthy home. Her mother and father worked hard to provide opportunities for their three daughters to be involved in sports, theater, and choruses. Their schedule was full of activities. At times, though, Caroline was not given the choice to disagree with participating in some of the activities, which resulted in more of a "go along to get along" strategy. Sometimes, she was encouraged to set aside her plans to allow for her siblings' agendas and to "quietly wait her turn."

Now, as an adult woman, the patterns of her childhood were repeating in her choices for partnerships. It was up to Caroline to speak up for herself as an adult and be clear about what she wanted.

The throat chakra, in its excesses and deficiencies, expands and contracts. Finding a healthy balance requires both speaking and listening. The timing of Caroline's breakup and the ensuing sadness was an opportunity to get quiet. The quiet was a chance for Caroline to listen . . . to herself.

What did *she* want?

We analyzed the steps necessary for Caroline to move forward in the direction of her wishes. I saw that the Washington Chorus, while respected and admired, also required a great deal of Caroline's time—several rehearsals a week and multiple performances on the weekends. It, too, began to feel like the demanding schedule she had grown up with. Subconsciously, Caroline was repeating the patterns of her childhood. I presented an alternative timeline to her.

"Caroline, you do not have to return to the chorus, if you don't want to. You can still serve your soul-purpose in a different manner."

For the first time in Caroline's adult life, she was given the space to identify what would feel healthy, exciting, and balanced for her. Next, it was up to her to speak it. By speaking it, she would activate the life force energy already within her to manifest the steps necessary to make it happen. For her second path, I saw that she would maintain her position at the bank and begin the process of offering voice lessons to children and adults. She would have complete control of her schedule, which would allow time for work, exercise, and a new love. Caroline was thrilled with this trajectory.

After our reading together, she quickly developed a website that claimed her repertoire and offered her services. She was speaking up about her wishes, listening to her heart's desire, and taking action to protect those ideals.

A few months into her new routine, the bank hired a new financial advisor to protect their customers' assets. In effect, Caroline had successfully applied the lesson and come into an alignment with her new love.

In the months that followed Caroline's reading, I kept thinking about what her guardian angels had shown me about *listening.* Not to her mother and not to her father and not to the music that surrounded her. But to the "still, small voice" within her.

REGRET

Cheryl James came through the back door of my office and paid for our session with cash. "I don't want my husband to know I am doing this," she said. "I don't think he would approve of it." I thanked her kindly and took her coat to hang on the hook by the door. Her eyes were puffy from crying and she walked with her shoulders rounded inward—to protect her heart. She placed an old-fashioned tape recorder on my office table and pressed RECORD. Her lips were pursed, and her arms folded across her chest, I thought to myself, *Why is she here, if she doesn't yet believe?* I began our reading, taking Cheryl's hands in mine, coming together with my opening prayer, and allowed her guardian angels and deceased family members to fill the room. She carried a gray cloud around her—one that I had become accustomed to seeing before. The gray cloud appears to me when someone is deep in the throes of grief and is a bit stuck in their sadness. Normally, a client scoots their chair closer to my table, but Cheryl remained distant and listened carefully as I opened the session. Her parents, who I named, were present, and I began narrating images of shared memories and experiences from her mother. I saw that Cheryl was building a new home, on a lake, and that the kitchen was currently being designed. Her mother encouraged her to have seven chairs, one for each family member, around the kitchen island. Cheryl's shoulders softened and she confirmed that yes, she is one of five children and in her mother's kitchen the table was always set for seven. As I continued to listen to her mom, additional family members stepped forward.

A young, charismatic man, tall and strong, stepped closer to me. I saw that he had crossed over abruptly, although not entirely as a surprise. I looked further into his energy and saw that he had become ill, due to his kidneys, and had neglected to seek medical attention even at the urging of his mother, Cheryl. Cheryl said, "Yes, Annemarie. I just knew he needed help and my intuition kept telling me to help him even more. But we ran out of time. There just was not enough time. I wish I had listened to myself more."

No one had expected that her son Patrick's kidneys would take an abrupt turn for the worse, sending him to the hospital. There, he experienced a stroke and remained unable to communicate until his unaddressed symptoms stacked against him, crossing him over without fair warning.

Cheryl was beside herself with regret and guilt that she had possibly overlooked key turning points in his illness. She had encouraged him to seek help, but her son Patrick had been resistant. Through my readings, I have observed that losing a child, be it an infant or adult, is no less painful. Parents of adult children struggle deeply with what they could have done differently to have changed the outcome.

I continued to work with Cheryl so she could connect with her beloved son. In our sessions, he often poked fun at the chores or projects that she delayed completing, or insisted on the vacations she take. While his physical body is resting now in peace, Patrick's spirit is thriving and is involved in Cheryl's life as ever. One of the aspects of his new commitment to his mother is to encourage her to learn that there is more to the Universe than what meets our physical senses. With every single session, Patrick says, "I love you, Mom!" and blows her a kiss.

Cheryl and Patrick's story combined elements of the throat and third eye chakras. The offerings of the sixth chakra teach us that while we cannot change the past, we can change our perception of the past. The first five chakras correspond to physical touch, smell, taste, hearing, and sight. In the sixth and seventh chakras, however, no physical senses correspond. Instead, rather, we cross the threshold from the sensations of the physical body and become more aware of the subtleties of the etheric field.

What we consume, eat, see, read, and who and what we surround ourselves with, create the grand total of our etheric field. When we start to understand the role of the third eye chakra, we begin to integrate the attributes of the physical realm into the sensations of the spirit.

AJNA
third eye chakra

6

THE THIRD EYE CHAKRA

> God is in everything I see
> because God is in my mind.
> —FOUNDATION FOR INNER PEACE,
> *A COURSE IN MIRACLES*

The third eye chakra is located in the center of your forehead. It is believed to be the singular point where the duality of the physical realm and the spiritual realm unite. It is here, in the third eye chakra, that we are able to access the higher degrees of consciousness. It is where we envision dreams and memories and our imaginative visions of the future begin to build.

X-RAY VISION

The daily conversations that I had with Arjun consistently had ample amounts of friendship, a drop of flirtation, and a healthy dose of spirituality. It was the perfect prescription for mind, body, and soul that kept my intrigue high. As friends do, we would jump back and forth from one topic to another. Should I shift my attention to the children or he to his patients, our conversations would pick up where they left off. We were both busy, both caregivers, and both healers—in our own unique ways. So, when Arjun had a particularly difficult case with a patient, it was only natural for us to discuss it. He had already witnessed my ability to see within the human body when we analyzed how his father crossed over, and we had created a trusted and confident bond, so I offered my help.

"Arjun, tell me your patient's first name, that's all I need—and I can take a look at what is going on within their energy and body."

Without any additional personal details, Arjun said his patient's first name: "Sharon." I began to clairvoyantly skip through images around his energy, like skimming names listed at the top of a phone book. I flipped the pages until I reached Sharon.

"Aha, yes I see her," I said, peering into the hologram. "She's mid-fifties, red hair, and her bowel is obstructed."

"Yes. That's her. That's why she came to me," he confirmed.

Together, we looked carefully into the trajectories for Sharon. I saw that she was surrounded by her angels, had severe abdominal distension, and her white blood cell count was elevated. She would require a second screening and it was imperative that she be screened for ovarian cancer immediately.

"Yes, this makes sense to me, Annemarie. I will call the hospital right away and get those tests ordered."

Arjun placed Sharon's case in the front of the line and results came back the following evening. He called me to thank me. "Annemarie, this is incredible. You were able to accurately identify beyond what we could see on her MRI and blood-work. Sharon is set to have her bowel obstruction cleared and we will ensure she meets with the right oncologist for her second chakra. Thank you."

I was so grateful to be able to assist Arjun with his work and, more importantly, get his patient Sharon to the care that was best for her. We began working together on cases that were especially difficult, patients that Arjun had not yet operated on as well as patients that required second surgeries. In the process, I was starting to learn more anatomy and more medical terminology. I felt like his work was very similar to mine. His patients came to him sick, injured, or just not feeling well. They sought his assistance and he utilized his education and experience to help them. Once he surgically opened his patients' physical bodies, he was able to see what was causing the issues and extract more information. The energetic field for me was just like the body to Arjun. Once I opened up a client's energetic field, I could see all of the internal structures and how each one affected the other. Together, we did amazing work.

Arjun was a patient teacher to me and often explained how the body works. I learned so much by observing the medical protocol and I gained even more respect for physicians. I believe he learned by listening to me about how the chakras work, too. Although, sometimes he would joke, "Chaka who? What? *Chaka Khan*?"

My confidence in medical intuition began to build. When I lacked the terminology, I would sketch what I saw—as my clairvoyance proved to be even more accurate than MRI or X-Ray machines.

Then, as the clusters of clients continued, several physicians started showing up as clients. In the privacy of their readings, we would take a clairvoyant look at difficult cases and unlock options that they may have overlooked. For example, I could pinpoint what medication was influencing the irregular heart rate for a patient of Dr. Diane's. Or help distinguish between undiagnosed HIV and the erratic symptoms of autoimmune disorders. I began to work closely with a transplant surgeon, as well. I could see in advance how her patients would respond to new organs—thereby preparing Dr. Isabelle for post-op recovery plans. It was an exciting time for me as a clairvoyant, and my third eye was in high gear.

Arjun and I saw each other often, and it seemed that the loving relationship that I had longed for was beginning to open. I had fallen in love with him and hoped that it would be reciprocated. One rainy spring day, we sat together in his car. As I waited for him to kiss me, he instead began speaking about his dad, fatherhood, and how "one day" he would like to be a father, too. "I'd make a pretty good dad, don't you think?" he asked me, and I nodded in agreement. He went on to explain that he would like to have his own children. My heart sank and anger sparked within me. I felt confused about his intentions with me now, as he implied that he would rather not have stepchildren, but children of his own. "Well, thank you for lunch, Arjun. I have got to get back to work." And I promptly stepped out of his car, into the rain, and slammed the car door shut!

I felt like such a fool and thought to myself as I walked into my office, *Oh, Annemarie. How could you be so stupid? He is just using you for your clairvoyance. Look how much you have helped his career! You are just filling his dance card until he meets a new woman that can offer him children. And then what?* I sat down at my desk and cried. I had given him so much of my time, my attention, and how could I have overlooked this?

I needed a time-out to get my emotions untangled. *We did work together so well. We did have chemistry. Didn't we?* It was a confusing time.

I recentered my attention on my work and children and put my readings with Arjun and my hopeful heart on the back burner. I thought about the chakras and how I could "get my joy up" as Candy would say. I enjoyed my clients and never even perceived it as "work," really, and fell back into the groove. It was a labor of love, and I was continuously humbled by the number of clients that continued to call. By the early months of 2019, my once get-up-and-go-ness had started to become a lot more like not-so-fast-ness, followed by crash-out for two days. I had been sick with what I thought was a terrible flu in 2018, for which I should have been hospitalized, but I decided to weather the storm at home—to be within reach of Christopher, Maria, and Anna.

It took several months to gain my strength back, but even into 2019, I was still not completely healthy. The kids were getting bigger, and the demands of their activities took over the calendar as I juggled clients in and around the flurry of sports, musicals, concerts, camps, birthday parties, holidays, and on rare occasions, vacations. I became accustomed to starting each conversation with my clients with, "Thank you for your patience . . ." I was back in the fast lane, but this time, driving the equivalent of an old Volkswagen bug.

I missed Candy and sought signs from her spirit routinely. I felt like *Top Gun*'s Maverick—"Talk to me, Goose"—when I was by myself seeking Candy's wisdom and compassion. *She'd know exactly what to do,* I often thought.

A committed romance with Arjun never got off the ground. It took time and much more quiet than I had expected to understand that he was right. I loved my three children more than anything else in the world. How could I possibly deny him the opportunity to have children of his own? Even if we did become a serious couple, I would not feel as though he would feel complete. Despite our constant connection, I began to back away. I had to let him go. I realized I did love him. And I loved him enough to let him go. Soon thereafter, he met a new woman and, just like I had intuitively felt, she was ready to start a family herself. Five months later they were married.

I have wished Arjun the best since then, and yet my heart called out for love. I found myself reminiscing about my very first love, Edward, and the summer we spent together in Italy. Yes, *Italy*! I replayed "what might have been" episodes in my imagination to help process my emotions. Was I digging up graves, so to speak? Maybe. I did not yet understand why these memories were resurfacing again like a grand review of the tragic story called "Annemarie's Unsuccessful Attempts at Relationships." Candy had instructed me that in order to see the future, we must first make peace with the past. If ever there was a lesson to my unrequited love, it was to let them go. *Let it all go.*

I sat with my heart in my hands for quite a while afterward. I ruminated. I turned things over and over again in my

mind. What could I have done differently? I prayed for a turning point or a beacon of light to look forward to. In the nick
of time, Jan called. She and Paul were preparing to host an
"Aura Photography" workshop back at The Inner-Connection,
and I registered to take the class. It would be good to learn a
new modality, visit with Jan, and be near the energy of Candy
again.

On the day of the class, Paul introduced the group to the
special equipment used to take pictures of electromagnetic
fields. One by one, each student was photographed, and the
picture was analyzed. I was able to see for myself my own
chakra system and where my energetic field was deficient or
excessive. Paul took my photograph in his hands and began
reading the images and interpreting the angels that were by my
side. It was amazing to see how small my heart chakra was in
comparison to the others. "Of course, it is, my dear," Paul said
supportively. "You've just had your heart broken, and it just
doesn't heal overnight, you know." He was right. For several
years since the divorce, I had armored up my heart, and had
not allowed myself to be truly vulnerable again in romantic
relationships. "Your throat chakra and your third eye, though,
ma'am, looks as though they're working overtime! Have you
thought about taking a break?" he asked.

"No, no breaks for me, Paul. I am happy to keep working,"
I said in defiance of my own heart's needs.

The Universe, though, had other plans for me. Summertime
had come and I was still not feeling like myself. No amount of
good food, running, yoga, Reiki, spending time with the kids, or
meditation seemed to work. I thought, *Maybe this is depression?*

It was as though each day I carried fifty-pound weights on my back and by mid-afternoon I was wiped out. I started to investigate further and visited several different doctors.

Mom said, "You're just getting older, Annie." But I knew that something was off. Even though I am a Medium and can see into the future, I am not omniscient. There are still many lessons for me to learn—this being one of them.

One sunny afternoon I was at the neighborhood park and had just rounded the third lap with our beloved border collie, when shooting pains like lightning bolts darted up my feet. After four or five more steps, it became too uncomfortable to walk, so I sat in the grass and paused. Which I never do.

I asked my body what it was trying to tell me. And all I could gather was "pause." *Pause? Pause for what? Pause? For how long?* I found it frustrating that I needed to be still. *There is so much work to do.*

The shooting pain subsided temporarily, but I made a phone call to Dr. Diane, my trusted friend and physician.

"Annemarie. Have you ever had a target-like rash on your body?"

"No. Never."

"Well, have you ever been bitten by a tick?"

"Oh, well, I may have. I came in from a run last year and found one on my leg, but I never had a rash."

"You do not need to have gotten a rash to have acquired Lyme disease. The pain in your feet sounds a lot like neuropathy, which can be from high doses of Lyme, left untreated."

The following week, the bloodwork Diane ordered proved,

in fact, that I had Lyme disease. Diane called again. This time she shared that it was the highest level of Lyme she had ever seen. I needed to start antibiotics right away.

I was grateful for the diagnosis and began the medication immediately. Diane mentioned that things could get worse before they got better, but I was looking forward to getting back to my old self again.

She was right, though. Things definitely got worse, and I landed sick in bed for two more weeks. *Pause! PAUSE! This is no pause!* I thought.

Messages at the office were starting to pile up and there was not an end in sight. So, I had to get honest with myself again. What was it that the Lyme needed to teach me? I knew how to apply the technique of the mirror—looking at the world around me as a reflection—but I had not experienced a lesson regarding my health.

The answer was simple: stillness.

When I attended my very first Reiki class and received my attunement, I had no idea that I had old emotions and irritations to release. That provided the example for me to base the Lyme process on. *Trust the process, right?* I recalled my grandmother Rita, being held back from school to recover from her illness. It felt like punishment to her at first, but she always looked back on that delay as a blessing. Had it not been for that sickness, she would not have had the opportunity to be alongside her mother before she crossed over. So, although the answer was not entirely clear, I trusted that I was in the right spot and that if the Universe needed me to sit still, I would. Like it or not.

I started moving clients to virtual sessions as best as I could. Some clients still preferred in-person sessions, but for the most part, everyone was just as happy to work together virtually. Soon, I figured out that by working from home, I was able to rest in-between sessions. Even saving the commute time added into my restoration. I thought seriously about letting go of the beautiful office on Market Street, and after much consideration, ended my lease agreement to have even more peace and quiet. I was sure these small adjustments would be temporary, though, until I was back on my feet again.

Then, without much warning, the entire world shifted. The pandemic in March of 2020 rearranged everyone's attention.

Now I knew the purpose of the stillness. *It was not for punishment, but for preparation.*

Quieter days ensued and the race to school and all the children's activities paused, too. This was truly a time-out. I began to write a little more, here and there, and I began to get greater downloads of information. I was understanding that the Lyme had been a temporary discomfort, but a long-term lesson. Stillness and peace became the intention behind every thought and action.

On the rare occasions when I was around people, I was clearer and clearer about the subtleties of energy. I recalled one of Candy's lessons: "Do not absorb. Observe." And I was able to see, for the first time, a direct result of staying in my awareness—without judgment. But, truly noticing just what I notice.

If the "eyes are the windows to the soul," then the third

eye is the window to consciousness. Since the third eye chakra and the crown chakra are so closely related, we can begin to understand that the third eye illuminates consciousness. It is not unlike me to need a wallop of a lesson, rather than a whisper from the Universe, and the Lyme provided just that. What I did not expect, however, was to be protected by it—through eliminating the overhead expense of the office just in time for the pandemic to shut down every business, big and small. I was grateful that the Universe had prepared me.

Seeing the signs is not always easy. No matter how integrated we are into the vibration of the Universe, we are still human! And it is easy to get caught up in the human experience. Reading the chakras is a wonderful way to interpret what is happening in our lives. We do not have to wait for a Medium to do that, however. Fortunately, signs come in all sizes, shapes, and colors and will naturally correspond to the chakra that is needing attention.

SMALL SIGNS: "WHISPERS"

I refer to the small signs from the Universe as "whispers." As long as we are paying attention, the whispers will catch our attention and draw our awareness to a situation that can be used for love or protection. It is safe to ask for guidance from your guardian angels and departed family members. They are as eager to invoke messages to you as you are to receive them.

Music is so important to me, and it is no wonder that the angels use songs to catch my attention most often. For example, the day that I finalized my divorce, I returned to my car, started the engine, and the song, "Joy to the World" by Three Dog Night was playing on the classic rock radio station. I sat back in the driver's seat, smiled, and knew my angels had my back. Music corresponds to the throat chakra and helps to keep our expressiveness alive and open. Listening to the lyrics of songs, or reading poetry, can help you to have an affirmation. Music also moves us to dance, and creative expression allows the sacral chakra to flow freely. Play an upbeat song to stir your creativity.

Animals come to me frequently as harbingers of what is to come. You do not have to be in wide-open places to see messages from animal spirits, either. I was stuck in New York City traffic not long ago and the delivery truck in front of me displayed a beautiful black horse raised on its hind legs—indicating to me to "keep charging ahead." Birds, especially, are messengers from angels and spirit. Have you been seeking peace and wisdom: the energy of the crown chakra? A visit from a dove will deliver just the affirmation you were looking for. Or have you been challenged by coworkers? The vulture makes you aware that not everyone has your best intention at heart. One client of mine had a hawk fly into his car and perch on his dashboard! Talk about getting your attention! Hawks have extraordinarily keen eyesight. The hawk's visit gave my client permission to move forward with a more spiritual perspective to living.

Synchronicity is often confused with coincidence. Have you ever been thinking of a person and a moment later, they call? Or, have you ever received the same present twice—from two different people? Synchronicities can be just the wake-up call needed to alert you to a hidden situation or an event that is to come. Synchronicities sometimes come in the form of stories, too. If John, Jim, and Jack have misplaced their keys, then I would suggest you hold on to yours! Are you paying attention yet?

Numbers are an ancient divination tool. Early on in my studies of signs from the angels and how they correlate to the chakra system, I discovered angelic numerology. This is a system of numbers applied to the chakra system for the purpose of a message from the divine. Each number, in sequential order, corresponds to a chakra. My interpretation is here:

7, 77, or 777—the crown chakra—When seeing these numbers, we are asked where can we apply a spiritual perspective? How can we see the bigger picture?

6, 66, 666—the third eye chakra—This is an invitation to look inward with compassion. We may be basing our choices on earthly ideals.

5, 55, 555—the throat chakra—Have we been speaking our truth? Have we been listening to ourselves honestly?

4, 44, 444—the heart chakra—How have we applied love to our experiences? To our relationships and ourselves?

3, 33, 333—the solar plexus—Where are we shining? How effectively are we using our power? And is it in congruence with love and creativity?

2, 22, 222—the sacral chakra—Is there a place in our life that we lack joy or pleasure? Is there a way we can creatively feel safe? Are we trusting?

I, II, III—the root chakra—Worries in the upper chakras cause us to cycle and recycle situations and relationships. How can you return your worries back to the earth? How can you ground? Where can you have faith?

> Now faith is the substance of things hoped for, the evidence of things not seen.
>
> —HEBREWS 11:1

If the whispers from the Universe have not caught your attention, or if you are doubting the signs, it is safe to ask for more and clearer signs. In prayer I will simply ask, "More, please, with grace and ease."

BIG SIGNS

Dreams are brought to you to help explore deeper meanings, visit with deceased family members, or have a foreknowledge about what is to come. The Universe wants us to be prepared and inspired. If we ask our guardian angels for guidance before falling asleep, expect the answer to come in the form of creative symbolism and vivid imagery in dreams. The third eye chakra and crown chakra correspond to dreams and déjà vu.

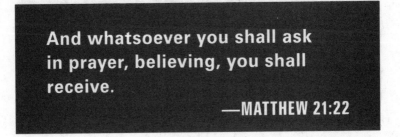

And whatsoever you shall ask in prayer, believing, you shall receive.

—MATTHEW 21:22

Déjà Vu is meant to alert your nervous system and set off an alarm within your awareness. Have you ever walked into a location and felt as though you had been there before? Have you ever held someone's hand, like I did with Arjun, and recognized their soul? Déjà vu helps us to know that what we are experiencing is right and true. Déjà vu corresponds to the throat chakra and helps to bring past-life stories, places, or relationships to our cognitive awareness.

Physical pain and illness are the biggest of the signs. Starting with something as simple as allergies, physical symptoms truly get our attention. Allergies, for example, ask us to think about what is "in our face, or under our nose" that we have not been able to see? Each chakra corresponds to where our ailment or illness rests in our body. One client reported experiencing a frozen shoulder, and received cortisone shots to reduce the pain and discomfort she chronically experienced. After taking a look at her heart chakra, I saw that her arm and shoulder "refused" to move as a means to protect her heart. Where are you experiencing discomfort or disease within your body? How can we consider the messages symbolically?

> And into the forest I go, to lose my mind and find my soul.
>
> —JOHN MUIR

SIGNS FROM NATURE

Nature has a myriad of signs that are associated with the chakras. For a very long time, I looked to the signs from Mother Earth to encourage me and continue to build my confidence. You may have guessed by now that my favorite signs are those of trees and flowers commonly found near my home and in my travels.

The root chakra is identified by the color red and is linked to chrysanthemum, amaryllis, and poppy flowers.

The chrysanthemum is the flower that I most associate with the root chakra. "Mums" are at their most vibrant hues in the autumn months near my home in the United States. Just when the leaves on the trees are changing to bright reds, too, the chrysanthemum invites us to celebrate transitions and take steps to move inward toward our roots for the coming winter months.

The amaryllis blooms in the coldest months of the year and is typically associated with the holiday season. Like the root chakra, the bulb of the amaryllis asks us to consider what is growing underneath the surface, while the remainder of the world is dormant.

The poppy is linked to sleep, rest, death, and the everlasting life. Its red hue is perfectly suited for the root chakra and is most frequently associated with remembrance and deep sleep.

The sacral chakra is identified by the colors of gold and orange and linked to the marigold, orange blossom, and carnation.

The marigold is associated with the second chakra's passion and center of creation. Once named for a substitute of gold, the marigold flower was an offering of hope, love, and devotion. Its name is a direct nod to Mother Mary, the mother of Christ.

The orange blossom is a beautiful and fragrant flower believed to attract the attention of a mate. It blooms in the springtime and is frequently used in bouquets, especially for the purpose of fertility and brides.

The long-lasting carnation is also associated with the sacral chakra as a runner-up to the rose to indicate romantic love and beauty. While the carnation comes in a variety of colors, the orange carnation is commonly used for the purpose of ornamental crowns and display and has been said to be named "God's flower."

The solar plexus chakra is expressed through the colors of gold and yellow. The flowers I associate with the third chakra are the sunflower, chamomile, and black-eyed Susan.

The tall and fast-growing sunflower symbolizes boastful pride in any garden. Celebrated by any admirer, the sunflower can also be symbolic of happiness, recognition, and attaining new heights.

Chamomile, with its lovely white flowers and peppy yellow center, calls to mind the solar plexus as both our center of energy and the center of our body and digestion. Chamomile and the essences of chamomile tea have been used for centuries to alleviate tummy troubles and disturbances with sleep.

The black-eyed Susan is a symbol of encouragement and at its height of bloom during the long days of summer symbolizes adaptability, transformation, and resistance to challenge.

The heart chakra is identified by bright greens and red through the hydrangea, the four-leaf clover, and the red rose.

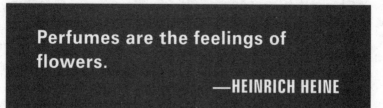

Perfumes are the feelings of flowers.

—HEINRICH HEINE

The limelight hydrangea is the hallmark of summertime blooms. Its cascading green petals symbolize gratitude, harmony, and grace.

The simplicity of the four-leaf clover is linked to the heart chakra by its color but also the four leaves—corresponding to the four chambers of the physical heart. Picking a four-leaf clover is believed to bring good luck and abundance.

The fourth chakra would not be complete without the red rose—symbolic around the world as the flower of romantic love. The heart chakra, however, is distinguished with more than one color, to indicate there is more than one kind of love. Red is associated with eros, or love and desire, and green is associated with agape, or love that is never ending.

The throat chakra is identified as blue and is symbolized by the flowers bluebell, periwinkle, and forget-me-nots.

The sensitive throat chakra is linked to the energy of the bluebell flower not just for its color, but also due to its ability to be overlooked. The bluebell flower grows close to the ground, can tolerate both sun and shade, and it is easy to step on, should it not be protected.

Periwinkle is also known as "star of the sea" due to its star-shaped center. Invoke the energy of the periwinkle flower to encourage thoughts and feelings to flow in your words like water in the sea.

The fifth chakra is associated with forget-me-nots as they are symbolic of telling stories and legends. In fact, forget-me-nots are believed to have begun when Christ wanted Mary to remember Him and blanketed the earth with the beautiful, delicate blue flowers.

The third eye chakra is symbolized by the color indigo and includes the flowers cosmos, purple rose, and the lotus.

The cosmos flower grows easily and often in the wild. It is most noted by its light purple color and willingness to thrive in forests, hills, and the countryside. The name itself means "universe."

The purple rose, also known as the "mystical rose," is exceptionally beautiful. It is associated with the feelings for "love at first sight."

The lotus flower, whose Hebrew name can be translated to "covering veil," is noted for its symbolism for transformation and purity. Perfect for the subtleties of the sixth chakra.

> ## The violets in the mountains have broken the rocks.
> ### —TENNESSEE WILLIAMS

The crown chakra is brilliantly identified through lilacs, lavender, and violets. These are the flowers I associate with the crown chakra for their well-known healing attributes and vibrant color.

The lilac flower, with its deep purples and lavenders, is emblematic of the crown chakra. It symbolizes purity of heart and connection to spirit. The Bible refers to the lilac with respect and admiration by saying that, "they neither toil nor spin."

Lavender is symbolic of purity, devotion, and silence. Lavender can be utilized for its soothing essence to calm the nervous system, rest, and rejuvenate. It correlates to balance.

Violets are best recognized for their sense of humility,

grace, and connection to spirit. As one of the flowers connected to the crown chakra, it is no surprise that it is symbolic of royalty and divinity.

"I SEE WHAT YOU MEAN."

I first met Claire through a virtual reading. She was seated at her home office desk with her camera narrowly focused on her face. She introduced her two beautiful German shepherds resting quietly at her side. She lived a few hours away from my office on the southern side of Washington D.C. but kept a very busy schedule as a nurse practitioner in palliative care. So, we scheduled her first reading around her limited availability.

I opened the reading by introducing her to her four guardian angels and defined what it meant for Claire to be an "earth angel." An earth angel is a person that has already committed to a soul-contract that agrees to work with lots and lots of angels in this lifetime. I went on to identify instances this lifetime where she had the free-will choice to make an alternative decision with her career but kept being called back to nursing. With each level of education, she thought about leaving nursing and opening a pet sitting or fostering business, but the financial security and benefits her employer provided were too much to risk losing. Not to mention, Claire's health had started to shift due to the demands of her full-time job.

I was shown that every time she moved forward with a new degree, she gained a little weight. Over time, the weight accumulated, and now, at forty years old, she felt trapped by the weight. She was often sad and lonely. She worried that her weight would prevent her from meeting a new love and getting married. She also worried that her beloved dogs were aging rapidly, and who would she come home to, once they were gone? It was definitely time for a transition out of the old ways of thinking and into the new.

These patterns were a cycle that Claire could not see her way out of. She had worked so hard to become a nurse practitioner. Now that she'd earned this role, she was so disappointed to realize that she was still left feeling unfulfilled.

In my readings with Claire, we worked together on defining her dreams and aspirations. Until recently, she had been so focused on attaining the next level of education, she had not really dreamed beyond that scope. At least not in a grounded manner. The weight that she had gained acted as a protective mechanism to assist her in staying grounded. Her guardian angels began to address Claire's limited perceptions around health and wellness, too. What we uncovered was that Claire's emotional health directly correlated to her physical health. As she neared the culmination of her degree, her physical body began to slow down as it approached the emotional risks of change. We spoke at length about illusions of happiness. I discovered that Claire was so committed to her work, she was self-sacrificing her own joy: essentially cutting herself short of life's joys. She began balancing her third eye chakra by imagining what joy would look like to her.

She had permission to be joyful.

We began to work backward. She wanted to be a homeowner with a large, fenced-in backyard. There, she envisioned that she would foster dogs and coordinate them with new "forever" homes. She started to look at the neighborhood that she was living in and realized that in order to attain the lifestyle she envisioned, she would relocate to the country. She began taking steps at creating an online presence where she could be more visible to the dog-fostering community. She also began to practice "seeing" solutions, rather than stopping when an obstacle arose.

Soon, she was sketching out the design of a dream foster-dog backyard and getting approved for a mortgage. Her role as a nurse practitioner proved to be the financial bridge necessary for her move. Once settled in her new town, she started to imagine the next step: a new job.

You can imagine that Claire's third step was to design and envision a new love, too. All that she visualized came to fruition. She was working beautifully in a new job, with a new home, with a new love. All because she imagined it and courageously took steps to manifest.

When I was working with Claire, I clairvoyantly saw that she'd had all of these trajectories available for quite some time. Many years, in fact. Her lesson, though, was to truly step into her dreams with courage.

SAHASRARA
crown chakra

7

THE CROWN CHAKRA

WHO DO YOU THINK YOU ARE?

I was seated at my desk in my office on Market Street when an old Toyota Corolla puttered into a parallel parking space, causing traffic to pile up. The driver, unaware, adjusted the angle of the car several times before coming to a complete stop. I remember thinking, *Geez, kid . . . you need more practice.* I watched as the young woman stepped out of the car, catching her skirt in the door, opening the door again to retrieve her skirt, and slamming the door closed again. Passersby honked as she appeared not to notice how close she was to the road. Hurriedly, she walked up the steps to my office and knocked on my door with a gentle tap. Opening the door, I introduced myself and reached out my hand to shake hers.

"Hello. I am Annemarie. Please, come in. You must be Willow."

"Yeah, um . . . hi . . . I am Willow. Should I sit here?" she said as she took off her cross-body purse and draped it over the back of her chair.

"Sure. Please make yourself comfortable."

It was May and all of the bright red roses were blooming out front. My office windows were open, and the church bells tolled as we sat down together for Willow's first reading. She was a gentle soul, with long brown hair that matched her name well. A friend had referred her to me so we could take a look, clairvoyantly, at her trajectories. Soon she would be graduating from high school, and she had no plans for her future.

Willow had only applied to one college in New England, and despite her grades being quite low, she was accepted. Her parents, however, refused to co-sign on the student loans because they lacked confidence in her choice of programs: art. Her father, a salesman, and her mother, a stay-at-home mom, had grown up locally and lived in the same town their entire lives. They did not feel the need for Willow to pursue a move and neither did they encourage her to consider alternative choices. They also did not approve of spending thousands and thousands of dollars on a degree that did not lead to a guaranteed career.

"Mom wants me to stay at home and start classes in the fall at the community college. She said my history with my grades has not proven to her that I can get through a semester. And why waste all that money?"

As with so many of my clients, I needed to understand some of the backstory so I could get an orientation for Willow. I clairvoyantly looked back in time and saw that her mother had, over the years, invited several tutors and support practitioners to help Willow with her academics. But Willow was not able to retain a lot of what she was learning. She was diagnosed with a learning disability and her parents began shielding her from taking risks as a means of protecting her self-esteem. "You just can't do those things," her mother would say again and again. And soon, Willow began to believe her.

The matter of attending college and the financial support was the symptom. But the limiting beliefs about Willow's intelligence and capacity to learn new things were the cause.

In order to move forward with grace and ease, I had to first share with Willow that part of her path now would be to begin to learn how to transcend what her parents wanted for her. And that it would be up to Willow to decide for herself, in a balanced and healthy manner, how to develop a belief about herself and a belief about her future that was not reliant on her parents' definition. Her parents loved her and cared for her but were basing their perspectives about Willow's choices on their own projections.

I needed to know "What is right for Willow?"

Her guardian angels surrounded her, and I looked to them to proceed. I knew that part of what Willow was working through was identifying her soul purpose, and finding the best way to step into that work. I saw that she was a hybrid soul—one that was both a teacher and a healer. I saw that her first "students" would be her parents. Willow would be teaching them how to define things based on intuition, rather than the traditional measures like grades, income, and material success. She had three distinct paths: the first path was to attend school in New England and foot the entire student loan on her own. The second path was to compromise by living at home with her parents, attend the local community college, and share the expense. And finally, the third choice was to move to a town nearby, begin working, and take classes toward a degree one by one.

Of all the paths, the third path had the most light and momentum. I saw that pursuing her degree one or two classes at a time would enable her to study at a comfortable pace. By working, she would gain some financial freedom from her family—thereby gaining self-respect and confidence. And by living independently, I saw that she would no longer remain under the type-casted role her parents had placed upon her.

I looked further out . . . two, four, six years, and saw that she would, in fact, choose the third path and settle into a small liberal arts college about two hours away. I saw her thriving while working at one of the college town's art galleries and taking classes, one by one, gaining momentum until she would earn a bachelor's degree in art education. Later, as an educator, she would work closely with students just like her that struggled academically. Her introduction to her work as an educator began by first learning what it felt like to be a student and to have her beliefs about herself compromised.

Willow listened carefully to the reading and said she would review the choices carefully before making her decision.

In October that year, I received a call from Willow requesting a virtual reading. Happily, I scheduled her and was excited to see what had transpired since we last met.

The second reading for Willow was much different than the first. She appeared grounded and engaged and was smiling as I viewed her through my computer. She was seated, criss-cross, on a futon in her new studio apartment. Panning her laptop around the room, she showed me how she had created space for an easel and painting supplies. Her favorite images to paint were the rolling green landscapes and flowers on her new college campus.

Her parents had willingly obliged to "give it a try" but agreed that she would return home if she began to fail any of her classes. Willow's first steps toward autonomy felt empowering and I could see right away that she would continue to succeed at school. She had chosen the third path and was thriving.

I was proud of Willow for having the courage to discuss her wishes with her parents. I know that it would be up to her to continue to design her dreams—because they were unique to her. Her parents' ambitions had been so different.

Limiting beliefs—be they intergenerational or from an active critical voice of your own—can come in the form of self-sabotage, skepticism, feelings of being overwhelmed, or relying on others to make decisions for you.

When my physician, Diane, has a particularly challenging case, we take a look in the privacy of her own readings as to how her patient's energy is through observing their chakras. When Sara Cato first registered for Dr. Diane's care, she had a litany of health issues to overcome. Diane's careful listening skills and gentle approach were just what Sara needed and before long all but one issue was resolved. So, Diane sent her my way.

When I first met Sara Cato, she gracefully and confidently

entered my office and sat down on the sofa, gently placing her purse on the floor. Her long blond hair and bright blue eyes gave her a California-girl glow. She was encircled with angels and immediately I knew she would be wonderful to work with.

Sara was already a master manifester. She meditated daily, prayed routinely, and was in constant contact with her guardian angels and support from spirit. Sara, who now had three young adult children, had begun working as a hairstylist while her children were in school and she moved through a divorce. Her warmth and kindness soon attracted more clients than she had room for, so she opened her own salon. "Sara's Salon" quickly became known as the best salon in town. As the salon grew, Sara hired the best stylists that resonated with her down-to-earth demeanor, and she happily committed to long hours with her team. Once a struggling single mom, she remained kind and empathetic, always keeping her clients' needs first, as the success started to build. Before long, Sara's work ethic brought clients to her salon from several hours away. Some booked months in advance for treatments with her or one of her team. Over time, she and her team helped thousands of clients; some through the loss of their hair from cancer treatments, some that were enduring domestic abuse or violence at home, and other clients that sought to create a whole new life after big changes. The success of her salon had positioned her for invitations to attend philanthropic events, receive awards, and grace the cover of popular industry magazines. Sara seemed to have the magic touch.

What is happening with her health that Diane could not figure out? I wondered.

"I'm ready, Annemarie. I don't know what it is, exactly. But I am ready for the next level. I feel excited and enthusiastic about the future. I want to help even more people. I just need to know where my guardian angels need me next."

Sara's sacral chakra was beautifully illuminated, and her guardian angels began to show me that there were many creative pursuits available to her, but first, she would be guided to pause, rest, and rejuvenate.

"Sara, Dr. Diane has sent you my way, so let's take a look at your health." I scanned her energetic field to see what was happening. Her angels immediately showed me that she needed a great amount of rest and quiet. A transformation was upon her.

Sara had no shortage of energy. But it was collected in her second chakra, as a way to clear it and make room for brilliant downloads of information that was on the cusp of being manifested. I clairvoyantly saw that, upon her recovery energetically and physically, Sara and Dr. Diane would go into business together. Utilizing the initial business model of the salon as a platform, they would open a wellness center that would offer head-to-toe wellness services encompassing physical, emotional, and spiritual practices. But, first, she had to rest.

"Your angels are indicating that it is time for a long period of rest, Sara."

"Ha! Annemarie, I am all for a vacation, but to really rest? I have worked so hard my entire adult life. I am not sure I know *how* to rest."

"Well, Sara, there's a reason that you are being called to take a pause," I said.

I saw that Sara had cysts resting in her ovaries that were stubborn and embedding into the lining of her uterus. "Yeah, they keep coming back," she confirmed, taking a deep breath.

"The cysts keep returning because there's a little more work to do in your sacral chakra. They're returning because there is unresolved trauma that is stored there. And before you are truly free to move forward, your angels are guiding you to take time for yourself to clear the energy of the past still resting in your sacral chakra."

"How do I go about doing that? I already meditate and walk."

"Yes, the best way to elevate your vibrations and get your chakras really aligned is to take a Reiki One class."

"That sounds wonderful. Please sign me up!" she said enthusiastically. And with that, Sara registered for a small Reiki One class at my office the following month.

On the day of the class, I introduced the history of Reiki, the Reiki principles, the chakras, and how to administer a Reiki treatment for yourself. At the end of the class, Sara received her Reiki One attunement, thanked me, and returned home to rest.

For Sara, the Reiki One attunement proved to be just what her emotional and physical body was seeking: a deep cleansing. Three weeks later, after daily self-Reiki treatments, she reported that she had sunk into a deep sadness and was reviewing her early childhood traumas. She decided to take a month away from her busy salon to process the spectrum of emotions that had been resting in her pain body and etheric field. Old traumatic feelings and images resurfaced, and she began working closely with Dr. Diane and a clinical therapist again for support. After several weeks, Sara returned for a second reading and a Reiki treatment. I saw that she was doing everything that she had been guided to do; rest, eat well, exercise, perform self-Reiki, and seek cognitive therapy and the support of her family. I also saw that she had an impending procedure that would remove the cysts in her second chakra once and for all. She expressed that she was nervous, but also wanted to clear her energy to make room for the next creative pursuits that she felt so passionate about.

The angels in her reading that day guided her to know that it was imperative that she rest. So, Sara and her husband decided to take a few more weeks away from the salon and rent a home in Florida for a month.

While in Florida, Sara rested more, ate well, laughed, spent time outdoors, and soaked up the sunshine. Sometimes, the soul needs more than a nap or a day of sleep. Sometimes, the soul requires peace. The peace she was able to access allowed her to meet her higher chakras, including her vibrant crown chakra. Her crown was ripe for downloads of information, ideas, and inspiration. Sara continued to stay in prayer and began to envision her next business opportunity: the wellness center.

"What if, Annemarie . . . what if Dr. Diane and I created a whole new wellness center like you saw in our reading? There's a need for the kind of care that she offers, and I have a ton of clients that would certainly respond well to her approach to clinical medicine!"

I knew that as soon as her body was ready, that Sara would connect the dots and she would move forward making this dream a reality.

THE CROWN CHAKRA

The crown chakra is located at the top of the head and is the connection between Heaven and Earth. The crown is where we review our dreams and visions that sparked in the third eye chakra and begin to bring the ideas into fruition.

The crown chakra is where we become illuminated as souls having a human experience. It is where consciousness resides within the physical body.

Sometimes, when we have limited ideas about our future or our goals, the energy from our chakras can be blocked or repurposed to another chakra temporarily. The crown chakra is also where we embody the wisdom and clarity that the remaining six chakras utilize.

When making choices from our highest chakra, the crown, we are making decisions that are best for the collective. The self is taken care of and feels fulfillment through the lens of service and honor to others.

In the case of Sara Cato, there is no limit as to what she can manifest next. I will be excited to see how the Universe aligns her path for her.

The day of my Kundalini Awakening was the day that my crown chakra opened. It was the culmination of the Shakti energy that began at my root and rose through my body and aura to the top of my head. Based on the spiritual experiences I had my entire life, I am grateful that it was not entirely open before. At thirty-five years old, I was finally mature enough to begin to take on the way of the spiritual warrior.

My father, a true warrior, instilled in me the value of courage. I believe that I inherited my courage from him. Like Dad, dyslexia found its way to me. When I was learning how to read and write, the letters and numbers often floated off the page. I developed a coping device by placing my hand on what I was reading to help me ground. I became a kinesthetic learner. Now, when offering a Reiki treatment, I use my hands to "see" the energy within my client. Growing up, though, my form of dyslexia was the least of my worries.

NOTICE WHAT YOU NOTICE

Over 25,000 clients have come to me for readings now. I look forward to working with every single new and returning client. And I am always excited to see where their guardian angels and family in Heaven guide them next and how their chakras have helped them thrive. Word-of-mouth referrals remain the dominant route for new clients to contact me for readings. When I first began to offer my readings formally, I often felt rushed to identify the information, images, and impressions that I was receiving. At first, the way in which I linked into Consciousness felt like racing alongside a moving train and hoisting myself up and on for the ride. I had to be in tip-top shape energetically to keep up. I was always guided by my angels, however, to interpret my readings in a manner that was appropriate for my client and move on to the next set of images. In some ways, it was like attempting to read the numbers and letters that floated off the page all over again! Readings were often like a wild and erratic rapid ride of information. It was overwhelming. And sometimes, it still is. The impressions will always be there, though, and part of my role as a Medium is to not pass any form of judgment, but to only notice what I notice.

Over time, I began to strengthen my ability to speak honestly and courageously with my clients. I never intended to offer my opinion—just deliver the messages.

Sometimes in my readings I am transported into an entirely new space. I remain seated on my chair in my office, in my body, but I can be in two places at once. I still see my client and the objects in my office, but a scene similar to a hologram superimposes the office. I narrate what I see and hear—details of a home, like the color and pattern on Grandma's kitchen wallpaper, the click of a temperamental lock on your old back porch door, the temperature in your childhood bedroom, or the smell of oil in your uncle's garage. Sometimes I physically sneeze in response to a dusty room and I always cough when I am "in" a room with a smoker. I have read posters that hang on bedroom walls and have seen the kinds of flowers in wedding bouquets. I have found missing jewelry and sacred family heirlooms. I have found underground streams and sketched out city streets and gardens in places that I have never seen before as far away as India. I take great joy and lose all sense of time when I am really focused in my readings. Dad would say, "Well, Annie, even a broken clock is right twice a day," but I smile knowing how he likes to keep me humble.

Sometimes, connecting to the energetic fields of others is not as easy as it may appear. Some clients have accumulated a great deal of emotional baggage that obstructs my connection, so I have more hurdles to jump over. Think of a busy train station where passengers are all headed in different directions, carrying heavy backpacks, purses, or carry-on luggage. Suitcases full to the brim! Now, imagine attempting to jump onboard a moving train while others are in your way, holding on to their baggage. This, I believe, is why some Mediums can get *some* information, but not the whole picture. This, too, is why I continue to learn how to keep my crown chakra open by a daily meditation practice.

IN GOD WE TRUST

Meditation keeps me grounded and allows for the light of consciousness to pour through my crown chakra. I have become sensitive to the activation of meditation and feel when energy that no longer serves me returns to the earth. Old energy rinses down my etheric field and returns to Mother Earth.

> **Stillness is the language God speaks, and everything else is a bad translation.**
> **—ECKHART TOLLE**

For me, meditation is the formless space where all ideas, feelings, information, and guidance are accessible. When I am meditating, I physically feel, from crown to root, a light pour over me and the weight of my worries begins to dissolve. I am reminded that I am not of this body, and not of this Earth. I remember that I am always connected to Source energy and I forgive myself for forgetting. Forgetting is inevitable and the point of being human. Then, I remember that forgiveness is not needed anyway because we are all children of God. God loves us unconditionally. God is love.

I began to understand that the entire world around me was mirroring my own energy. The clusters of clients were just the first pattern that I picked up on. Then, I became aware of similar patterns amongst my peers. Finally, I saw how the lessons I had been resistant to continue to show up in my romantic relationships. So, I began to take another honest look at the most important relationships in my life. I realized that I was still not being as clear as I could be with regards to my own wishes. I was still making assumptions. I realized, too, that I still needed firmer boundaries with others, and myself. Again and again, I practice the mantra of "reveal, review, release." I ask myself, *What can I learn by interacting with this person? What are they showing me through their beliefs, their words, or their actions that are resting within me that I have yet to reveal to myself? What stirs low vibrational feelings like shame, anger, sadness, or grief within me?*

8

ENLIGHTENED

Since the beginning of time, stories have been passed down from one generation to the next about the great themes that we, as humans, attempt to understand. Over time, science and communication have allowed for an expansion to our understanding and awareness of life around us and within us. It is only a natural evolution to continue to progress toward a greater good. As we move forward in the direction of unconditional love for each other and ourselves, we may do so by first allowing for the dissolution of the past.

The Sanskrit word "aparigraha" means to let go of attachments. While I did not realize it at the time, the clusters of clients influenced me to understand my own healing and recovery while moving me in the direction of my soul purpose work. When I recall the Kundalini Awakening in the fall of 2011, I realize now that it was the physical awakening of what I had been born to do. It gave me permission to allow for new thought systems and to make room for the higher consciousness that was like a springtime sapling bursting through the earth. Over the course of time, I was guided to keep letting go of the past, letting go of illusions, letting go of my pain body, letting go of limiting beliefs, and letting go of expectations.

> **If you realize that all things change, there is nothing you will try to hold on to. If you are not afraid of dying, there is nothing you cannot achieve.**
>
> **—LAO TZU**

Working so closely with death and dying has offered me a close-up perspective of transitions. In truth, we all die many deaths in one lifetime. I was once the bright-eyed little girl that played with dolls and teddy bears with her beloved sister, Jenny. The restless and moody music-loving teenager. The adventurous sailor and the determined student. The loyal wife. The doting young mother. None of these exist anymore, however none of them are gone, either. Show me a Mr. Potato Head and I will gladly giggle through a pretend drama with Mrs. Potato Head. "Oh, how are you, my handsome spud!" Or, I will lace up my running shoes and go on a run with my children and you will find a competitor that still calls cadence. However, now, in my middle age and mindful as to how my energy influences my body, my home, my children, and my work, I employ all that I have learned through the clusters of clients, the letting go, and the chakras to prepare for more transitions to come and my highest potential.

> My God, a moment of bliss. Why, isn't that enough for a lifetime?
> —FYODOR DOSTOEVSKY

What is our highest potential? There were moments following my Kundalini Awakening when time slowed down and I was keenly aware that I was experiencing something phenomenal: bliss. Bliss is a limitless marvel, where we experience God and perceive the Earth through absolute and unconditional, all-encompassing love. It is a miracle.

Bliss is a state that everyone has the ability to access, however not all know that they have the ability to do so.

To offer a simplified example, it is similar to chocolate. How do you know you like chocolate if you have never tasted it? A chocolatier may attempt to describe the taste, the smell, the texture—but until you have tried it yourself, you just will not know.

You have got to give it a try. There is a space, I believe, between the vision of bliss and the application of it. Within that space we must first come to the need or the willingness to dare. In my case, it was a need. I knew I could no longer fit within the limitations of my family's generational expectations or my misguided and exhaustive direction of light within my marriage. Some may claim a mindful approach to correcting their path. I like to refer to it as both mindful and accountable. I am accountable for my life and the legacy I choose to leave.

As you develop your awareness of the divine within you and around you by utilizing the chakra system, you will experience the dichotomy of the earthly experience. The push and pull of the past, karmic relationships that come and go to offer sacred lessons and expand and refine our understanding of love, as well as a disciplined need for openness and a stillness in your day-to-day life.

Now, if you could, apply my example by utilizing the chakras as a means to access your bliss. Like the Spruce Street mystic told me, I will tell you: you will lose everything. You will lose your fear of living a life that was not intended for you. You will lose doubt. You will lose worry. You will lose illusions and lies. You will lose misperceptions. You will lose your beliefs that are no longer serving you. And you will lose any inkling of separation from yourself and the divine.

You will come to feel safe in your own divinity. In your own creativity. In your own power. In your own love. In your own expression. In your own phenomenal vision.

Your bliss is your divine right. There is no secret, really, but the Universe is whispering to us all now, "Follow the signs." God is in everything—Divine Intelligence that is ever giving, ever and all-knowing—and we are constantly co-creating with this eternal Source. You are that same Source: you are enlightened.

PRACTICE

Many times, I sought a reference or validation for the spiritual experiences that I was having personally or professionally. I thought you would benefit by having a practical guide to your enlightened being. While the process is generalized, your outcome will be unique. You will know you have attained an enlightened state when you feel peaceful and when you have a depth of gratitude for the relationships that have shaped your experiences, knowing that each one has served, or is serving, a purpose.

Here are seven steps that you may apply to your own life as influenced by the seven chakras.

STEP ONE: SAFETY

The physical body is powerful, and once it is safely anchored, more light and love may pour through the body and expand outward. I associate a sense of safety with getting grounded. I commit to my practice of staying grounded daily; however, I recommend that you listen for what works best for you and your body.

Mantras—Mantras are wonderful tools that can be practiced anywhere. A mantra can be recited throughout the day, as a strategy to bring you to your center or to simply focus on your breath. For the root chakra you may place your hand on your heart, or the earth, take a deep breath in, and exhale slowly. Then say, "I AM SAFE."

Meditation—A guided meditation may bring your awareness out of the physical world and into your inner world. Please go to AnnemarieHeckert.com for a guided meditation from me to you for your root chakra.

Movement—Walking or running are wonderful ways to ground, but I have found that the best movement for a sense of safety is yin yoga. Yin yoga is a slow-moving yoga that may be practiced in your home on a yoga mat or blanket. It is intended to offer compassion and ease. Child's pose, butterfly pose, and corpse pose are three simple options for both beginners and advanced yoginis. Children to mature adults may choose to stay in each pose for up to five minutes, or combine all three poses for a fifteen-minute practice.

Music—You may create a playlist that speaks to you with songs that inspire a sense of safety, family, tribe, and connection. Or you may try some of my favorites!

> Johann Sebastian Bach, "Cello Suite No. I in G Major"
> The Dixie Cups, "Iko Iko"
> The Five Stairsteps, "O-o-h, Child"
> Etta James, "I Got You Babe"
> Ben E. King, "Stand by Me"
> Sister Sledge, "We Are Family"
> Stevie Wonder, "Don't You Worry 'Bout a Thing"

STEP TWO: CREATIVITY

Once grounded and feeling safe, give yourself permission to allow inspiration to guide you. The sacral chakra corresponds to creativity, creation, passion and intimacy, flowing emotions, and movement.

Mantra—For the sacral chakra, place your hand on your

heart, or your lower abdomen between your hips and your navel, take a deep breath in, and exhale slowly. Then say, "I AM CREATIVE."

Meditation—A guided meditation may bring your awareness out of the physical world and into your inner world. Please go to AnnemarieHeckert.com for a guided meditation from me to you for your sacral chakra.

Movement—Any movement that begins with the hips and radiates joy will stimulate the sacral chakra. It is no surprise that dancers are typically tapped into their creativity and share multiple modalities of expression such as singing or playing instruments. You too may enjoy dancing or try three more yoga poses on a yoga mat or blanket: happy baby pose, pigeon pose, and goddess pose.

Music—You may create a playlist that speaks to you with songs that inspire a sense of creativity, passion, excitement, and joy such as:

David Bowie, "Let's Dance"

Leon Bridges, "River"

James Brown, "Get on the Good Foot"

Louis Fonsi, "Despacito"

Marvin Gaye, "Let's Get It On"

Louis Prima, "Pennies from Heaven"

Robert Randolph & The Family Band, "The March"

STEP THREE: POWER

Everything that you do, feel, say, and believe is a negotiation in your personal power. Like beams from the sun, the solar plexus radiates our power and is the source of our intuition. It is where we digest our feelings and connect to our heart above and earth below.

Mantra—For the solar plexus, place your hand on your heart or your stomach, take a deep breath in, and exhale slowly. Then say, "I AM POWERFUL."

Meditation—A guided meditation may bring your awareness out of the physical world and into your inner world. Please go to AnnemarieHeckert.com for a guided meditation from me to you for your solar plexus.

Movement—The solar plexus helps us to feel self-motivated with a sense of purpose and power. High-intensity training, running fast paced or sprinting, as well as these three yoga poses will activate your solar plexus: triangle pose, boat pose, plank pose.

Music—Lighthearted or hopeful, commanding or capable, the solar plexus offers opportunities for radiance.

The Beach Boys, "Good Vibrations"
The Beatles, "Here Comes the Sun"
The Byrds, "Turn! Turn! Turn!"
Sam Cooke, "A Change Is Gonna Come"
The Edwin Hawkins Singers, "Oh Happy Day"
Alicia Keys, "Girl On Fire"
Buddy Miles, "Them Changes"

STEP FOUR: LOVE

The heart chakra will prove to be the litmus test of your well-being. Here, you will discover that emotions come and go, but *you* are not your emotions. You will begin to experience observing your emotions as they are part of the physical experience and you will develop a love that includes compassion, kindness, forgiveness, and acceptance for yourself. You will give this love and receive this love equally.

Mantra—For the heart chakra, place your hand on your heart, take a deep breath in, and exhale slowly. Then say, "I AM LOVING." Next, place your hand on your heart, take a deep breath in, and exhale slowly. Then say, "I AM LOVED." Repeat these two steps as many times as necessary until you feel centered in this truth.

Meditation—A guided meditation may bring your awareness out of the physical world and into your inner world. Please go to AnnemarieHeckert.com for a guided meditation from me to you for your heart chakra.

Movement—The heart chakra gives and receives just as we inhale our breath and exhale. Naturally, the lungs correspond to the heart chakra. Cardiovascular exercise such as biking, hiking, running, swimming, or walking are excellent sources of energy to restore or open your heart chakra. Also, you may try these three yoga poses for the heart chakra: cobra pose, cow pose, warrior pose.

Music—

Performed by Adele, written by Bob Dylan, "Make You Feel My Love"

Nat King Cole, "L-O-V-E"

The Drifters, "This Magic Moment"

Aretha Franklin, "Baby, I Love You"

Alison Krauss, "I Will"

Elvis Presley, "Can't Help Falling in Love"

Righteous Brothers, "Unchained Melody"

STEP FIVE: EXPRESSION

The throat chakra is said to be our sword. The tongue has the capacity to cut ties, uphold boundaries, or protect our heart below and head above. The more you practice being "impeccable with your word," or to "just for today, be honest," the more you will feel centered in your heart as well as your mind. Likewise, you will clearly hear others as well as yourself.

Mantra—For the throat chakra, place your hand on your heart, your throat, or your ears, breathe in, and exhale slowly. Then say, "I AM EXPRESSIVE."

Meditation—A guided meditation may bring your awareness out of the physical world and into your inner world. Please go to AnnemarieHeckert.com for a guided meditation from me to you for your throat chakra.

Movement—Any form of creative expression is an extension of the throat chakra. Acting, dancing, drawing, painting, playing an instrument, singing, writing, or listening to stories or music are all excellent practices for the throat chakra. Author Julia Cameron encourages a daily "Morning Pages" journaling practice in her book *The Artist's Way*. Notice how your day reflects honesty and authenticity after journaling in the morning. For an added benefit, add these three yoga poses: cat pose, camel pose, and plow pose.

Music—Songs that you feel comfortable humming or singing along to are great choices for the throat chakra.

Ray Charles, "What'd I Say"

Earth, Wind, and Fire, "Sing a Song"

Ella Fitzgerald & Louis Armstrong, "Cheek to Cheek"

Tommy James & the Shondells, "Crystal Blue Persuasion"

Elton John, "I Guess That's Why They Call It the Blues"

Chaka Khan & Rufus, "Tell Me Something Good"

Bonnie Raitt, "Something to Talk About"

STEP SIX: PERSPECTIVE

The third eye chakra invites us to stay present or look forward with our sight. As multidimensional beings, it is safe and wonderful to look to the future, reflect upon the past, peer into our innermost desires, or dream for what may come.

Mantra—For the third eye chakra place your hand on your heart or over your eyes, breathe in, and exhale slowly. Then say, "I AM PERCEPTIVE."

Meditation—A guided meditation may bring your awareness out of the physical world and into your inner world. Please go to AnnemarieHeckert.com for a guided meditation from me to you for your third eye chakra.

Movement—It is not enough to simply have dreams. The third eye chakra, combined with the resources of your solar plexus and root chakras, are the perfect combination for manifesting! To manifest is to bring your dreams into fruition. You may begin by creating a vision board. Write down specific words, draw or cut out pictures, and place them on a board that you see daily. You may refine over time what is included on the vision board; however, make note each time you have manifested one image. For example, cut out a picture of a person looking peaceful, or images that resonate with you that represent clarity such as blue skies or indigo-colored flowers.

Music—For the third eye, you may be drawn to songs that validate the complexities behind the scenes or inspire your vision to come true.

The Allman Brothers Band, "Dreams"

Krishna Das, "Om Namah Shivaya"

George Harrison, "My Sweet Lord"

The Manhattans, "Shining Star"

Joni Mitchell, "Both Sides Now"

Van Halen, "Dreams"

The Who, "Behind Blue Eyes"

STEP SEVEN: WISDOM

The crown chakra is our connection to source energy and is sensitive to all the physical body's subtleties. To activate your crown chakra is to integrate the physical realm with the Heavens.

Mantra—For the crown chakra, place your hand on your heart or on top of your crown, breathe in, and exhale slowly. Then say, "I AM KNOWING."

Meditation—A guided meditation may bring your awareness out of the physical world and into your inner world. Please go to AnnemarieHeckert.com for a guided meditation from me to you for your crown chakra.

Movement—As we have ascended through the body, so too

have we ascended in vibrational frequency. In doing so, we are capable of receiving more, while doing less. For your seventh chakra, you will find that a quiet space where you feel comfortable is best for a meditation—this time, unguided. For the best results, meditation between you and source energy can be practiced daily. At first, you may commit to three minutes, gradually staying in your quiet and comfortable space a little longer. Notice what you notice without judgment or question. As my guardian angels requested of me, I will suggest to you one word: "Allow."

Music—You may discover that your connection with spirit is beyond all form, reason, or language. You may feel particularly connected with songs that have few lyrics, but convey a breadth of emotion, nonetheless.

Samuel Barber, "Adagio for Strings"
Samuel Barber, "Agnus Dei"
Claude Debussy, "Claire De Lune"
Yo-Yo Ma and Kathryn Stott, "Over the Rainbow"
Yo-Yo Ma and Kathryn Stott, "The Swan (Saint-Saëns)"
Pink Floyd, "Great Gig in the Sky"
Deva Premal, "Gayatri Mantra"

RECOMMENDED READING

A New Earth by Eckhart Tolle

A Return to Love by Marianne Williamson

Anatomy of the Spirit by Caroline Myss

The Artist's Way by Julia Cameron

The Four Agreements by Don Miguel Ruiz

The Subtle Body, An Encyclopedia of Your Energetic Anatomy
   by Cyndi Dale

Wheels of Life by Anodea Judith

You Can Heal Your Life by Louise Hay

SELECTED BIBLIOGRAPHY

Andrews, Ted. *Animal-Speak: The Spiritual & Magical Powers of Creatures Great & Small*. (Woodbury, MN: Llewellyn Publications, Llewellyn Worldwide, 2002).

Dale, Cyndi. *The Subtle Body: An Encyclopedia of Your Energetic Anatomy*. (Boulder, CO.: Sounds True, Inc., 2009).

Hay, Louise. *You Can Heal Your Life*. (Carlsbad, CA: Hay House, 1984).

Judith, Anodea. *Eastern Body, Western Mind: Psychology and the Chakra System as a Path to Self*. (New York: Random House Inc., Celestial Arts, 2004).

Judith, Anodea. *Wheels of Life, A Classic Guide to the Chakra System*. (Woodbury, MN: Llewellyn Publications, 1987).

Karlsen, Kathleen. *Flower Symbols: The Language of Love*. (Bozeman, MT: Living Arts Enterprises, LLC, 2011).

Myss, Caroline. *Anatomy of the Spirit: The Seven Stages of Power and Healing*. (New York: Crown Publishers, Harmony Books, LLC, 1996).

Ruiz, Don Miguel. *The Four Agreements: A Practical Guide to Personal Freedom*. (San Rafael, CA: Amber-Allen Publishing, 1997).

Stein, Diane. *Essential Reiki: A Complete Guide to An Ancient Healing Art*. (New York: Random House, Inc., Crossing Press, 1995).

The New Testament of Our Lord and Savior Jesus Christ with Psalms and Proverbs. (Philadelphia, PA: National Publishing Company, 1968).

Tolle, Eckhart. *A New Earth: Awakening to Your Life's Purpose*. (New York: Penguin Group, Plume, 2006).

Williamson, Marianne. *A Return to Love: Reflections on the Principles of A Course in Miracles*. (New York: Harper Collins, 1992).

ABOUT THE AUTHOR

ANNEMARIE HECKERT is a world-renowned clairvoyant Medium, Reiki Master, and Registered Yoga Teacher. Born with the natural ability to communicate with angels and spirits, Annemarie offers private sessions, events, and workshops at her office in central Pennsylvania as well as virtual sessions for clients around the globe. She has held over 25,000 consultations to date. When not working, Annemarie enjoys spending time with her three children and their beloved border collie. *Enlightened* is her debut book.